SPECTRUM

5

A Communicative Course in English

Sandra Costinett
with *Donald R. H. Byrd*

Donald R. H. Byrd *Project Director*

Anna Veltfort *Art Director*

Prentice Hall Regents
Upper Saddle River, NJ 07458

Library of Congress has cataloged this title as follows
Costinett, Sandra
    Spectrum 5, a communicative course in English/ Sandra Costinett
with Donald R.H. Byrd; Donald R.H. Byrd, project director;
Anna Veltfort, art director.
      p. cm.
      ISBN 0-13-830191-3
    1. English language—textbooks for foreign speakers. I. Byrd
Donald R.H. Byrd II. Title. III. Title: Spectrum five.
PE1128.C7257 1994   94-5482
428.2'4—dc20   CIP

© 1994 by PRENTICE HALL REGENTS
Prentice Hall, Inc.
A Paramount Communications Company
Upper Saddle River, New Jersey 07458

Printed in the United States of America

10 9

Project Manager: Nancy L. Leonhardt
Manager of Development Services: Louisa B. Hellegers
Editorial Consultant: Larry Anger
Contributing Writer: Gerry Strei
Audio Development Editor: D. Andrew Gitzy
Assistant to the Editors: Jennifer Fader
Reading Researchers and Writers: Sylvia P. Bloch, Randee Falk, Virginia Lowe
Director of Production and Manufacturing: David Riccardi
Editorial Production/Design Manager: Dominick Mosco
Production Editor and Compositor: Paula Williams
Page Composition: Ken Liao, Steve Jorgensen
Electronic Production Coordinator: Molly Pike Riccardi
Production Coordinator: Ray Keating
Production Assistant: Wanda España

Cover Design Coordinator: Merle Krumper
Cover Design: Roberto de Vicq
Electronic Art: Todd Ware, Rolando Corujo

Interior Concept and Page-by-Page Design: Anna Veltfort

ISBN 0-13-830191-3

PRENTICE-HALL INTERNATIONAL (UK) LIMITED, *LONDON*
PRENTICE-HALL OF AUSTRALIA PTY. LIMITED, *SYDNEY*
PRENTICE-HALL CANADA INC., *TORONTO*
PRENTICE-HALL HISPANOAMERICANA, S.A., *MEXICO*
PRENTICE-HALL OF INDIA PRIVATE LIMITED, *NEW DELHI*
PRENTICE-HALL OF JAPAN, INC., *TOKYO*
PEARSON EDUCATION ASIA PTE. LTD., *SINGAPORE*
EDITORA PRENTICE-HALL DO BRASIL, LTDA., *RIO DE JANEIRO*

REVIEWERS AND CONSULTANTS

For the preparation of the new edition, Prentice Hall Regents would like to thank the following long-time users of
Spectrum, whose insights and suggestions have helped to shape the content and format of the new edition: Motofumi
Aramaki, Sony Language Laboratory, Tokyo, Japan; Associacão Cultural Brasil-Estados Unidos (ACBEU), Salvador-
Bahia, Brazil; AUA Language Center, Bangkok, Thailand, Thomas J. Kral and faculty; Pedro I. Cohen, Professor
Emeritus of English, Linguistics, and Education, Universidad de Panamá; ELSI Taiwan Language Schools, Taipei,
Taiwan, Kenneth Hou and faculty; James Hale, Sundai ELS, Tokyo, Japan; Impact, Santiago, Chile; Instituto Brasil-
Estados Unidos (IBEU), Rio de Janeiro, Brazil; Instituto Brasil-Estados Unidos No Ceará (IBEU-CE), Fortaleza,
Brazil; Instituto Chileno Norteamericano de Cultura, Santiago, Chile; Instituto Cultural Argentino Norteamericano
(ICANA), Buenos Aires, Argentina; Christopher M. Knott, Chris English Masters Schools, Kyoto, Japan; The Language
Training and Testing Center, Taipei, Taiwan, Anthony Y. T. Wu and faculty; Lutheran Language Institute, Tokyo,
Japan; Network Cultura, Ensino e Livraria Ltda, São Paulo, Brazil; Seven Language and Culture, São Paulo, Brazil.

SPECIAL ACKNOWLEDGMENTS FOR LEVEL 5

Kevin McClure, ELS, San Francisco, CA; Elise Klein, ELS, New Haven, CT; Robin Fraatz, ELS, Oakland, CA.

INTRODUCTION

Welcome to the new edition of *Spectrum*! *Spectrum 5* represents the fifth level of a six-level course designed for adolescent and adult learners of English. The student book, workbook, and audio program for each level provide practice in all four communication skills, with a special focus on listening and speaking. Levels 1 and 2 are appropriate for beginning students and "false" beginners. Levels 3 and 4 are intended for intermediate classes, and 5 and 6 for advanced learners of English. The first four levels are offered in split editions — 1A, 1B, 2A, 2B, 3A, 3B, 4A, and 4B. The student books, workbooks, audio programs, and teacher's editions for levels 1 to 4 are also available in full editions.

Spectrum is a "communicative" course in English, based on the idea that communication is not merely an end-product of language study, but rather the very process through which a new language is acquired. *Spectrum* involves students in this process from the very beginning by providing them with useful, natural English along with opportunities to discuss topics of personal interest and to communicate their own thoughts, feelings, and ideas.

In *Spectrum*, comprehension is considered the starting point for communication. The student books thus emphasize the importance of comprehension, both as a useful skill and as a natural means of acquiring a language. Throughout the unit students encounter readings and dialogues containing structures and expressions not formally introduced until later units or levels. The goal is to provide students with a continuous stream of input that challenges their current knowledge of English, thereby allowing them to progress naturally to a higher level of competence.

Spectrum emphasizes interaction as another vital step in language acquisition. Interaction begins with simple communication tasks that motivate students to use the same structure a number of times as they exchange real information about themselves and other topics. This focused practice builds confidence and fluency and prepares students for more open-ended activities involving role playing, discussion, and problem solving. These activities give students control of the interaction and enable them to develop strategies for expressing themselves and negotiating meaning in an English-speaking environment.

The *Spectrum* syllabus is organized around functions and structures practiced in thematic lessons. Both functions and structures are carefully graded according to level of difficulty, and usefulness. Structures are presented in clear paradigms with informative usage notes. Thematic lessons provide interesting topics for interaction and a meaningful vehicle for introducing vocabulary.

This student book consists of twelve units. Each unit begins with a preview page that outlines the functions/themes, language, and forms (grammar) in the unit. Preview activities prepare students to understand the cultural content of the readings that begin each unit and give them the opportunity to draw upon their own background knowledge. The first lesson in each unit establishes the theme with a reading selection. Students read authentic newspaper or magazine articles that have been carefully adapted for use in *Spectrum*. The articles are accompanied by a variety of as-you-read and follow-up activities that develop reading skills. The next lesson presents a realistic conversation, providing input for comprehension and language acquisition. New functions and structures are then practiced through interactive tasks in a three-page thematic lesson. The next two-page lesson includes discussion or role-playing activities that draw on students' personal experience, and a listening exercise related to the theme of the unit. The final lesson of the unit presents a variety of situations, photos, artwork, short articles, or listening passages as springboards for writing practice. There are review lessons after units 6 and 12. An accompanying workbook, audio cassette program, and teacher's edition are available.

SCOPE AND

S E Q U E N C E

LANGUAGE	FORMS	SKILLS
What made you decide to go into medicine? I'd always wanted to be a doctor, even as a child. On another occasion, a moose had thought that it was cornered. . . . It was so hot (that) I couldn't run. It was such a hot day (that) I couldn't run. It's too hot to run. He doesn't run fast enough to win. But you haven't been running long enough to enter a race! I didn't know enough English to understand a lot of questions.	The past perfect *So* and *such* with result clauses *Too* and *not . . . enough* with infinitives	Listen to people talk about past or continuing events Write a paragraph
I need your advice on something. Some friends of mine are coming to town for the weekend and I don't have any idea where to take them. I'd suggest going to the flea market. Speaking in public makes me nervous. It makes me nervous to speak in public. I'd suggest signing up for a course in public speaking. In the United States, you should always ask your host before you take a friend along to dinner. In my country, you must always give taxi drivers a tip. Tips are a big part of their salary. Really? You must be on time. We mustn't be late for dinner.	Gerund vs. *it* as subject *Must* and *mustn't* for obligation and prohibition vs. logical conclusion	Listen to people talk about rules of social behavior Write an answer to a letter asking for advice
Our course will help you get over your nervousness. We'll have you write speeches and then we'll let you try them out on your classmates. Most important, we'll make you realize that you can be an effective speaker. In my opinion, children need responsibility. If parents have children help with chores, the children will feel needed. What's more, they will learn to take care of themselves.	*Have*, *make*, *let*, and *help* The definite article *the*	Listen to people trying to persuade others Write a response to a letter
When my brother and I were growing up, we used to spend summers with my grandparents in Brazil. Every morning we'd walk through the market place. When my grandfather was a boy, he lived on a farm. I used to be very interested in philosophy. I never got tired of talking about the meaning of life. Now I don't have time to worry about such things. I'm more interested in practical problems.	The past habitual Some verbs and expressions followed by prepositions	Listen for responses Write about a childhood memory
What a strange experience that must have been! How incredible! A toymaker climbed the World Trade Center yesterday. He'd never climbed it before. He was climbing the tower when the police arrived. I saw the water rising. I heard my friend scream.	*How . . . !* vs. *What a . . . !* The simple past vs. the past perfect vs. the past continuous Sense verbs with base and progressive forms of verbs	Listen to people tell stories Write a newspaper article
How come you've stopped taking English? Well, I'd really like to continue taking it, but I'm too busy this month, so I think I'll wait until next semester. Since it's such a beautiful day, why don't we do something outdoors? I hope Joan isn't sick. I wish Joan weren't sick. I hope my boss will give me a raise. I wish my boss would give me a raise.	Conjunctions *so*, *because*, *since*, *even though*, *although*, and *though* *Hope* vs. *wish* in present and future time	Listen to people talk about their hopes and wishes Write a letter
Review	Review	Review

ACKNOWLEDGMENTS

ILLUSTRATIONS

Pages 7, 21, 24, 69, 88, 89, 90, 91, 130, and 136 by Anna Veltfort; pages 34, 36, 40, 46, 73, 102, 103, 122, 124 (bottom), 131, and 132 by Anne Burgess; page 72 by Rolando Corujo; pages 8 & 9 (background), 31, 38, 39, 61, 76, 77, and 109 by Hugh Harrison; pages 1, 4, 23, 50, 57, 92, 105, 112, 113, and 128 by Randy Jones; pages 10, 18, 19, 41, 44, 60, 62, 64, 66, 74, 75, 79, 82, 94, 95, 124 (top), 125, 126, 127, and 134 by V. Gene Myers; pages 26, 45, 98, 110, 111, 115, and 118 by Charles Peale; pages 11, 51, 58, and 59 by Janet Pietrobono; pages 14, 48, 49, 96, and 97 by Bot Roda; pages 16, 17, 54, 78, 83, 85, 93, 104, and 114 by Arnie Ten.

PHOTOS

Page 2 by Jeff Schultz/Alaska Stock; page 5 (left) by Barbara Alper/Stock Boston; page 5 (middle) by Gale Zucker/Stock Boston; page 5 (right) by Chester Higgins Jr./Photo Researchers, Inc.; pages 8, 9 and 12 by Frank Labua; page 20 by Donald Miller/Monkmeyer Press; page 28 (top) by Lionel Delevingne/Stock Boston; page 28 (left) by Paul C. Margolis Phototography; pages 28 (middle), 29 (top right), 30 (center), and 80 by Peter Menzel/Stock Boston; page 28 (right) by David Heald/Solomon R. Guggenheim Museum; page 29 (top left) by United States Steel; page 29 (middle left) by AppaLight; page 29 (middle right) by Peter Southwick/Stock Boston; page 29 (bottom left) by Toni Michaels/The Image Works; pages 29 (bottom right), 86 (top) and 87 (middle) by Bob Daemmrich/The Image Works; page 30 (top) by Grant, Spencer/Monkmeyer Press; page 30 (bottom) by David Simson/Stock Boston; page 32 by Jerry Howard/Stock Boston; page 33 by Albert Coya/Miami Herald; page 35 by James R. Holland/Stock Boston; page 37 by The Bettmann Archive; page 39 by Paul Conklin/Monkmeyer Press Photo Service; page 42 by Barry Staver/*People Weekly*; page 47 by Jack Prelutsky/Stock Boston; pages 53 and 129 (left) by AP/Wide World Photos; page 55 (left) by Owen Franken/Stock Boston; page 55 (middle & right) by Rhoda Sidney/Picture Person Plus; page 65 by Ira Wyman/SYGMA; page 66 by Charles Marden Fitch/FPG International; page 68 by Ed Reinke/AP Wide World Photos; page 71 (top) by Alexander Tsiaras/ Science Source; page 71 (bottom) by Chuck Wyrostok/AppaLight; page 71 (middle) by AT & T; page 81 (middle) by George Bellerose, Stock Boston; page 81 (bottom) by David J. Same/Stock Boston; pages 86 (bottom) & 87 (top right & bottom right) by Mitch Wojnarowicz/The Image Works; page 87 (top left) by Elizabeth Crews/Stock Boston; page 87 (bottom left) by Stock Boston; page 100 by UPI/Bettmann; page 106 (top) by Gregory Schwartz/Photofest; pages 106-108 by Photofest; pages 119, 120, and 121 (left) by Reuters/ Bettmann; page 121 (right) by L. Rorke/The Image Works; page 129 (right) by Ancil Nance/ Allstock; page 133 by *People Weekly*.

REALIA

Pages 3, 5, 6, 20, 22, 26, 32, 33, 42, 43, 66, 67, 70, 74, 80, 81, 95, 96, 97, 99, 100, 120, 121, 129, 131, 133, 134, 135, and 136 by Siren Design; pages 47, 52, 56, 60, 62, 63, 65, 66, 67, 70, 78, 84, 90, 98, 115, 123, and 125 by Anna Veltfort.

PERMISSIONS

Pages 2-3: "Arctic Adverntures," by Larry Mueller from *Outdoor Life*, reprinted with permission of Larry Mueller and Times Mirror Magazines © 1991. Page 13: © 1983 by The New York Times Company. Reprinted by permission. Page 22: Reprinted with permission of Peter Muller. Page 32-33: Reprinted with permision of *People Weekly* © 1991, Time Inc. Page 42-3: Reprinted with permission of the Los Angeles Times Syndicate ©1991. Pages 52: Reprinted with permission of *Smithsonian* and Roderick MacLeish ©1989. Page 61: ©1983 by The New York Times Company. Reprinted by permission. Page 63: © 1984, USA TODAY. Excerpted with permission. Page 67: © 1984, USA TODAY. Excerpted with permission. Page 80-81: © 1983 by The New York Times Company. Reprinted by permission. Page 90: © 1983 Reprinted by permission of Rodale Press, Inc. Pages 110-111: Excerpted with permission of *People Weekly*, Febrary 21 © 1983, Time Inc. Pages 116-117: © World Copyright by Quino. Page 131: © 1984, USA TODAY. Excerpted with permission. Page 133: Excerpted with permission of *Newsweek*, ©1991. Page 135: Reprinted by permission of the Associated Press.

The editors have made every effort to trace the ownership of all copyrighted material and express regret in advance for any error or omission. After notification of oversight, they will include proper acknowledgement in future printings.

P R E V I E W

FUNCTIONS/THEMES	LANGUAGE	FORMS
Talk about a decision	What made you decide to go into medicine? I'd always wanted to be a doctor, even as a child.	The past perfect
Tell a story	On another occasion, a moose had thought that it was cornered. . . .	
Emphasize something	It was so hot (that) I couldn't run. It was such a hot day (that) I couldn't run.	*So* and *such* with result clauses
Give a reaction Tell about a past experience	It's too hot to run. He doesn't run fast enough to win. But you haven't been running long enough to enter a race! I didn't know enough English to understand a lot of questions.	*Too* and *not . . . enough* with infinitives

Preview the reading.

1. Discuss these questions in small groups.

   a. Have you ever been in a race? What kind of race was it? Did you win or lose? How did it feel to win or lose?
   b. Why do people challenge themselves? Do some people take too many risks when they challenge themselves in sports or other activities?

2. Before starting to read the article on pages 2–3, look at the photos and the title of the article. What do you think the article is about? Now read the italicized sentence under the title. Did your answer to the question change?

1.

Arctic Adventures

Not only have Susan Butcher and her sled dogs won the Iditarod Sled Dog Race on four occasions, but they've also beaten death.

Susan Butcher called her sled team to a quick halt in the black of night about 150 miles out of Anchorage. A cow (female) moose stood blocking the trail ahead.

"This has happened before," Butcher thought, optimistically. "We'll deal with it."

Butcher was eager to move on. This was the Iditarod Sled Dog Race from Anchorage to Nome, and she was mushing (driving) her best team in seven years. Butcher had already set a new time record for the first leg of the trip, and her chances of winning had never been better. But an Alaska, moose can be highly dangerous. Butcher would give this one all of the time she needed to move.

And she did move! The moose turned and charged straight into the dog team. Butcher reached for the .44-caliber handgun usually kept in the sled, then remembered she hadn't packed it. There was only the ax. Without hesitation, she grabbed the ax, and in her words, "went after the moose." Incredibly, she succeeded in driving the animal out of her team, but not before some of her dogs had been severely injured.

Instead of leaving, however, the moose charged back into the team. Again Butcher approached the moose, swinging her ax. This was not simply a valuable team and her best chance of a win, these dogs were her closest friends. Two were already dead. Butcher swung with a fury. Oddly, all the while that Butcher fought for her dogs' lives, her thoughts were also in sympathy with the moose. "My God she's so skinny! She must be starving to death!" And very likely it was starvation that made this moose behave as she did. She may have perceived the dog team to be a pack of wolves. Her instincts may have told her that she was too weak to escape by running. Her only chance to survive would be to drive off the "wolves," which, of course, were harnessed together and couldn't run away.

After 20 minutes of fighting, Butcher noticed the flash of a headlamp coming up from behind. "Moose!" she yelled long before her fellow musher got close enough to be in danger. "Tie your team. Do you have a gun?"

Susan Butcher's adventurous attitude has led her to take some incredible risks.

Susan Butcher and dog team.

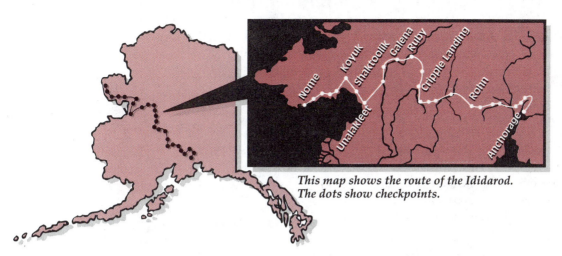

This map shows the route of the Ididarod. The dots show checkpoints.

"Yeah!" The other musher tied his team to a tree and ran up to shoot the moose. But it was too late to save Butcher's team for this race. Besides two dead, 13 more dogs were injured.

On another occasion, Butcher risked her life when she decided to mush across 40 miles of sea ice. All went well for 30 miles until Butcher neared the cliffs that she had been told to avoid. Suddenly, she could feel the roller-coaster sensation of ice moving beneath her feet.

Instinctively, Butcher called, "Haw," to her lead dog, Granite. He obediently turned left toward shore, but the ice billowed upward, then fell apart as it dropped back down—dumping dogs, sled, and Butcher into 30 feet of water so cold it can be survived for only minutes. Granite struggled to reach solid ice, then dug toenails into the slick surface to pull himself and his partner out of the water. Two by two, the rest of the team followed until the sled and Butcher were pulled from the sea.

Unwilling to trust the ice again, Butcher guided her team onto the beach. The dogs could survive the minus 15°F (minus 9°C) with ease. Their coats were water-resistant. Butcher was, however, soaked to the skin. Hypothermia was a serious threat. But she handled it with her typical optimistic attitude, running behind the sled to get warm and thinking, "This isn't too terrible. If it was minus 30°F (minus 36°C) or worse, I'd have to do something different."

Butcher has overcome these and other life-threatening situations to win the Iditarod four times. Like any genuine adventurer, she thoroughly enjoys winning against incredible odds.

Figure it out

1. **While you read the article, try to figure out the answers to the questions below. Do not stop to look up new words until you've finished the article. Then adjust your answers if necessary.**

   1. What is the Iditarod Sled Dog Race? How would you describe a sled-dog race to someone?
   2. What is difficult about a sled-dog race?
   3. What is Susan Butcher like? What clues does the article give about her personality?

2. **Put these sentences in the correct order as they occur in the article. Then use them and any other information you need to summarize the story briefly in your own words. Make sure to say whether or not Susan Butcher finished the race.**

   - _6_ 1. The other musher ran up and shot the moose.
   - _4_ 2. The moose charged back into the team.
   - _2_ 3. A cow moose turned and charged straight into Butcher's dog team.
   - _3_ 4. Butcher grabbed an ax and went after the moose.
   - _1_ 5. Susan Butcher started out on the Iditarod Sled Dog Race.
   - _5_ 6. Butcher warned a fellow musher about the moose.

3. **Many words in English can be used as either nouns or verbs with no change in spelling or form. (However, sometimes the pronunciation changes.) Find forms of the words below in the article, and say if they are used as nouns or verbs.**

   1. trail _N_
   2. deal _V_
   3. move _V_
   4. race _n_
   5. record _n_
   6. chance _n_
   7. pack _V_
   8. escape
   9. drive _V_
   10. run _V_
   11. flash _n_
   12. trust _V_

Compare:	
Noun	*Verb*
récord	recórd

2. You made it!

1. The 10-kilometer "Run for Your Life" marathon, held every year to raise money for heart disease research, is about to begin. You are a reporter covering the event, and your partner is one of the runners. Interview the runner. Start by asking how long he or she has been running. Then ask other questions, using *ever* and *before this*.

Have you ever run in a marathon before this?

🔲 A TV reporter is interviewing Meg Harmer, who just finished last in the "Run for Your Life" marathon.

Listen to the conversation.

②

Reporter Well, here comes the last runner to cross the finish line . . . . You made it!

Meg Yeah!

Reporter How does it feel?

Meg Great! I mean, it's not everyone who comes in last.

Reporter You look pretty tired.

Meg I am, but I'm so excited I don't think I'll be able to get to sleep for a while.

Reporter Was this your first race?

Meg Yes. I've only been running for two months. When I signed up, I'd only been running for two weeks! Everyone said it was too soon to enter a race.

Reporter Well, you certainly showed them! Was there ever a time when you thought you would drop out?

Meg Well, it was such a hot day that I started feeling a little tired pretty early. And I hadn't even gone three miles when I got a pain in my side.

Reporter How was that last big hill?

Meg Oh, that was a killer. I'd just made it about halfway when my right knee started giving me trouble. I didn't know if I had enough energy to get to the top. But I managed to do it.

Reporter What made you decide to enter the race?

Meg Well, I'd always wanted to see if I could make it through a race like this. Besides, I knew they'd give me one of those cute T-shirts.

Reporter Well, I guess I should say "Congratulations for hanging in there!" Thanks for talking to us. This is Vince Edwards for KITV.

3. Complete the sentences with *I've*, *I'd*, *I haven't*, or *I hadn't*.

1. ___I've___ been running for two months and I really enjoy it.
2. ___I'd___ been running for two weeks when I entered the race.
3. ___I hadn't___ even run three miles and I'm already tired.
4. ___I hadn't___ even run three miles when I got a pain in my side.
5. ___I've___ always wanted to run in a race, but I just never have.
6. ___I'd___ always wanted to run in a race, until I sprained my ankle.

3. I'd always wanted to be a doctor.

1
- ▶ Listen to the interviews.
- ▶ Interview a classmate. Ask questions about your partner's life, past and present. Find out about a decision your partner has made and the situation that led up to it. Use the expressions in the boxes.

What made you decide to go into medicine?

Well, I'd always wanted to be a doctor, even as a small child. My mother was a doctor, and so was my grandfather.

What made you decide to drive a truck?

I'd just finished high school and I needed a job. And I'd never been anywhere outside my hometown.

What made you decide to change careers?

I'd been working at the same job for fifteen years, and one day I just woke up and said, "Enough!"

What made you decide to . . .	Well . . .
go into business for yourself?	I'd always heard. . . .
major in mathematics?	I'd just taken a course. . . .
move to the city?	I'd lived in a small town since. . . .
take up running?	I'd been thinking about it for. . . .

You *go into* a profession, *major in* a school subject, and *take up* a sport or leisure activity.

---

2 ▶ Study the frame: The past perfect

I You He She We They	had ('d)	**wanted**	to be in a race.
		been	in a race before.
	hadn't	**run**	three miles when Jane hurt her knee.

▲ past participle

'd = had
hadn't = had not
I'd = I had *or* I would

Notice how past perfect questions are formed.

Had you ever been in a race before?
Hadn't you finished school when you got this job?

Notice how the past perfect continuous is formed.

How long had you been studying English when you went to London?
I'd been taking English in school for ten years.

Use the simple past or present perfect to refer to a situation or event in the past.

I got my first job three years ago. (a specified time in the past)
I've already finished school. (at an unspecified time in the past)

Use the past perfect to emphasize that one event in the past occurred before another.

I'd already finished school when I got my first job.
(First, I finished school. Then I got the job.)

Use the present perfect to refer to something that began in the past and continues into the present.

I've always enjoyed running.

Use the past perfect to refer to something that began in the past and continued until another point in the past.

I'd always enjoyed running until I entered my first race.

---

3 ▶ Listen to the runners in the "Run for Your Life" marathon. Is the first speaker in each conversation talking about an activity that continues into the present or one that ended in the past? Check (√) the correct column.

	Continues into the present	Ended in the past
1.	✓	
2.		∿
3.		
4.		
5.		

4 ▶ **Use the past perfect and the sentences in the box to describe what happened to Susan Butcher before the Iditarod Sled Dog Race ended.**

Start like this:

Butcher had set a new time record for the first leg of the race.

- Butcher set a new time record for the first leg of the race.
- The moose turned and charged straight into the dog team.
- Butcher reached for the .44-caliber handgun usually kept in the sled.
- There was only the ax.
- Incredibly, she succeeded in driving the animal out of her team.
- Instead of leaving, however, the moose charged back into the team.
- Again Butcher approached the moose, swinging her ax.
- A fellow musher shot the moose.

5 ▶ **Study the frame: *So* and *such* with result clauses**

So and *such* with result clauses			
It was	**so hot** **such a hot day**	(that)	I couldn't run.

so + adjective
such + adjective + noun

 6 ▶ **Listen to the conversation.**
▶ **Act out similar conversations, using the facts in the "Strange But True" column. Use *so* or *such* in each conversation.**

A Hmm . . . I didn't know this. There's a disease that's call laughing sickness.
B Oh, come on now! I find that hard to believe.
A No, really. It's so rare that it only affects one tribe in New Guinea.

Some ways to start
Hmm . . . I didn't know this. Listen to this. . . . Did you know that . . . ? I was just reading that . . .

Some reactions
Oh, come on now! I find that hard to believe. Yes, I've heard that. No kidding! That's interesting. Now that you mention it, I think I read about that.

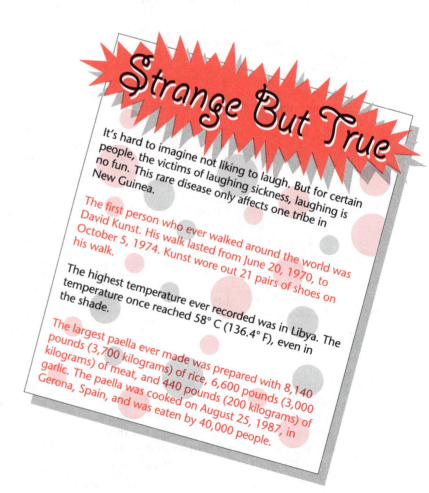

Strange But True

It's hard to imagine not liking to laugh. But for certain people, the victims of laughing sickness, laughing is no fun. This rare disease only affects one tribe in New Guinea.

The first person who ever walked around the world was David Kunst. His walk lasted from June 20, 1970, to October 5, 1974. Kunst wore out 21 pairs of shoes on his walk.

The highest temperature ever recorded was in Libya. The temperature once reached 58° C (136.4° F), even in the shade.

The largest paella ever made was prepared with 8,140 pounds (3,700 kilograms) of rice, 6,600 pounds (3,000 kilograms) of meat, and 440 pounds (200 kilograms) of garlic. The paella was cooked on August 25, 1987, in Gerona, Spain, and was eaten by 40,000 people.

7 ▶ Study the frames: *Too* and *not . . . enough* with infinitives

It's	**too** hot		**run**.	◄	*too* + adjective or adverb
He doesn't run	fast **enough**	to	**win**.	◄	adjective or adverb + *enough*

There were	**too** many people		**see** anything.	◄	*too many* + count noun
It takes	**too** much time	to	**walk** there.	◄	*too much* + mass noun
I don't have	**enough** energy		**run**.	◄	*enough* + count or mass noun

8 ▶ **In the conversations below, restate the second speaker's reaction so that it includes either *too* or *not . . . enough* and an infinitive.**

1. **A** I think I'll enter the "Run for Your Life" marathon.
   B But you've only been running for two weeks!
   But you haven't been running long enough to enter a race!

2. **A** Janet and I would like to get married.
   B But you're only seventeen years old!

3. **A** How did you do on the test?
   B Not too well. There were a lot of essay questions that we had to answer.

4. **A** Let's get a bite to eat before the play.
   B It's already after seven. The play starts at eight.

5. **A** What did you think of the new Kurasawa movie?
   B We were sitting so far back that we couldn't read the subtitles.

6. **A** How was the lecture?
   B I was so exhausted after work that I couldn't even pay attention.

I think I'll enter the "Run for Your Life" marathon.

But you haven't been running long enough to enter a race!

9 ▶ **Write a paragraph about a personal experience that was frustrating, disappointing, or difficult in some way. Explain why, and then tell about the situation that led up to the experience. When you have finished, share your experience with another student.**

Last summer, I went to the United States to study English. After I registered in the program, I had to take a placement exam. I had just arrived in the United States the day before, and I was so tired I couldn't keep my eyes open. I hadn't studied much English yet, and I didn't know enough English to understand a lot of the questions.

Some topics	
an exam	your driving test
a class	a job interview
an embarrasing social situation	a contest or competition
a problem with a boyfriend/girlfriend	a foolish financial decision

4. Your turn

It's 6:00 in the evening and you are riding the train. There are many different kinds of people on the train with you, and as you look at them, you wonder how they spent their day and what their lives have been like. Look at the people in the photos, and then work in groups to make up stories about some of them. Consider each of these questions.

1. Where is the person going and what had the person been doing before he or she got on the train? Are there any clues in the photo?
2. What sort of lifestyle does the person have? What made him or her decide to choose this lifestyle?
3. Has the person made a big decision recently? If so, what led up to it?
4. Has something exciting, interesting, important, disappointing, or sad happened to the person recently? If so, what led up to the event or situation?

🔲 Listen in

Read the statements below. Then listen to two conversations taking place on the train and say *Right* or *Wrong*. Correct the wrong statements.

Conversation 1
Nancy
____ got a job.
____ didn't get a job.
____ got a raise.

The company
____ didn't interview anyone but Nancy.
____ interviewed three people.
____ had already hired someone else.

Conversation 2
Bill
____ decided to change colleges.
____ had discussed his plans with his parents before he dropped out of school.
____ kept the same schedule he had before he quit school.

5. On your own

1. Your local newspaper has a weekly column called "Slice of Life." In it, the paper prints interesting stories about people. Write a story for the column about someone on the train from exercise 1 on page 8. You may write one of the stories your group made up or you may write about someone else.

2. Write a story about what happened in each of the pictures below. Tell what happened at the time of the picture and what had happened before that. Compare your stories with your partner's stories.

FUNCTIONS/THEMES	LANGUAGE	FORMS
Ask for and give advice	I need your advice on something. Some friends of mine are coming to town for the weekend, and I don't have any idea where to take them. I'd suggest going to the flea market. Speaking in public makes me nervous. It makes me nervous to speak in public. I'd suggest signing up for a course in public speaking.	Gerund vs. *it* as subjec
Talk about customs	In the United States, you should always ask your host before you take a friend along to dinner.	
Talk about social rules	You must be on time. We mustn't be late for dinner.	*Must* and *mustn't* for obligation and prohibition vs. logical conclusion

Preview the reading.

1. Work with a partner. Look at the pictures and discuss your likes or dislikes for the different food items shown. Then talk about the dishes from your country which you like the most and the least.

2. Before you read the article on page 13, look at the title and the photos on page 12. Then work with your partner and try to guess the answers to these questions.

   a. People around the world eat with their hands, chopsticks, or forks. Where is each way most popular?
   b. When and why were chopsticks and forks invented?
   c. How have people's attitudes toward the three ways of eating changed over time?

6.

Fingers, Chopsticks, or Forks

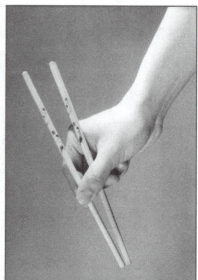

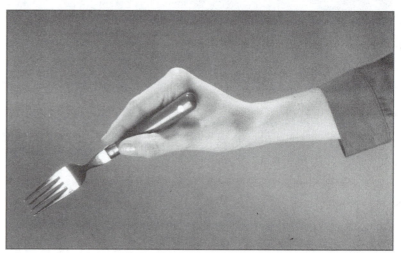

Figure it out

1. Read the article. Then check your answers to the questions on page 11. If necessary, correct your answers.

2. Read the article again and try to figure out the main idea of each paragraph. When you have finished reading, choose *a* or *b* for the paragraphs below.

1. Paragraph 3:
   a. Throughout most of history, people have eaten with their fingers.
   b. Some people used to think the fork was evil.

2. Paragraph 7:
   a. Sailors in the British Navy ate with their fingers.
   b. Until fairly recently, the fork was not completely accepted in Europe.

3. Paragraph 8:
   a. Only Westernized people continue to eat with forks.
   b. Finger-feeding is starting to grow in many areas of the world.

1 All the world is divided into three parts—finger-feeders, chopstick-feeders, and fork-feeders. Why people fall into these categories, however, is a mystery.

2 Fork-feeders are most numerous in Europe, North America, and Latin America; chopstick-feeders in most of eastern Asia; and finger-feeders in much of Africa, the Middle East, Indonesia, and India. This means that fork-feeders are outnumbered two to one.

3 Fork-users have historically been in the minority. People have eaten with their fingers for most of human existence. As little as three centuries ago, most Western Europeans still used their fingers. French historian Fernand Braudel tells of a preacher in Germany who lived during the Middle Ages. The preacher thought the fork was evil and called it a "diabolical luxury; God would not have given us fingers if he had wished us to use such an instrument."

4 Forks and chopsticks won favor because they made it easier to handle hot food. Before these instruments, people usually ate hot food with a piece of flat bread. The exception was in China, where flat bread was probably not eaten.

5 According to Dr. K. Chang of Harvard University, Chinese food was served in small portions which did not require cutting with a knife or fork. There was, however, a need for food to be carried from the bowl to the mouth, and chopsticks came along to meet that need. Some of the oldest Chinese chopsticks date from 1200 B.C.

6 The fork made its way to Western tables several hundred years later, but it was not immediately accepted. Forks were used for many years in Europe and the Near East, but only as kitchen implements. The general use of forks as eating utensils started with the Byzantines in the tenth century A.D. (The Byzantine Empire extended through southeast Europe, southwest Asia, and northern Africa, including what is now Greece and parts of Turkey, Italy, and Egypt.) The first illustration of their use at meals was in a manuscript from the monastery of Montecassino in Italy in 1022 A.D.

7 Although the fork entered society on the tables of the rich and well-born, many members of royalty, including Elizabeth I of England and Louis XIV of France, ate with their fingers. When Napoleon III of France, a fork-man, met the Shah of Persia, a finger-feeder, they strongly disagreed about the correct way of bridging the gap between plate and mouth. As late as 1897, sailors in the British Navy were not permitted to use knives and forks because using them was considered unmanly.

8 Not only has finger-feeding withstood the passage of time, but some scholars believe that it may be enjoying a comeback. This is because the areas with the highest birthrates do not use forks. In most of these finger-feeding areas, only Westernized people see forks as status symbols and continue to use them. Finger-feeding is growing with each new generation.

9 What is the best way of getting food into the mouth? There is a lot of disagreement on the topic. Those who use one utensil often think people who don't are uncivilized or even barbaric. And anyone who has ever eaten at a formal table elaborately set with many different kinds of knives, spoons, and forks can sympathize with Oscar Wilde, who said, "The world was my oyster, but I used the wrong fork."

---

3. The prefix *out-* can be put before a verb to mean "to do something more than, better than, or longer than." Complete each sentence, choosing the appropriate verb below. Make sure to use the correct form of the verb.

outdistance   outgrow   outlive   outnumber   outweigh (be more important than)

1. In the last mile, the runner *outdistance* three other racers and finished second.
2. Unless I start taking better care of my health, my parents might *outlive* me.
3. Finger-feeders *outnumber* fork-feeders two to one.
4. My children *outgrow* their clothes so fast that I have to buy new clothes every month.
5. When you're having dinner with someone and trying to make a good impression, table manners can *outweigh* conversation and personality.

7. I need your advice.

1. You are invited to a formal dinner in a classmate's country, and you want to make a good impression. Ask your classmate for advice on what to do and what not to do.

Victor and Elena Santana are having dinner at Bob and Ann Colemans' house. Victor notices two sets of chopsticks on the table.

Listen to the conversation.

---

②

Ann Come on, let's sit down and eat.

Victor Low on forks? I would have been happy to bring some.

Bob No, no, we're just practicing our chopstick technique.

Ann A Japanese couple is having us over for dinner next week.

Bob One thing I'll say for these things is I don't eat as much. It's too hard to get the food to my mouth.

Ann Especially those little grains of rice. I had to practice long and hard to manage those.

Elena Bringing the bowl to your mouth makes it easier. In fact, it seems to me I read somewhere that it's considered very rude not to.

Ann It's so easy to offend people when you don't know their customs. I remember one time a friend of mine from Switzerland had us over for dinner.

I baked a cake for dessert. Later I found out you're not supposed to take your host any food.

Elena They must have thought you were terribly rude.

Ann I'm sure they did, but they were too polite to say anything.

Bob Listen, I need your advice. Do you think we should take our Japanese friends something?

Elena Well, I wouldn't suggest taking food. . . . You could take something for their kids.

Bob Good idea. . . . Are we supposed to bow, do you think?

Victor Now wait. . . we *are* in the United States. . . .

Elena I don't think you have to bow. But remember, you must take off your shoes.

Victor And you mustn't wear socks with holes in them.

Ann Now there's some good advice!

---

3. Match.

1. I wouldn't suggest baking a cake.
2. Do you think we should bake a cake?
3. They must have baked a cake.
4. You could bake a cake.
5. You must bake a cake.

a. ask for advice
b. give advice
c. state an obligation
d. reach a conclusion

8. I'd suggest going to the flea market.

1 ▶ **Listen to the conversation.**

▶ **Act out similar conversations with a partner. Ask your partner for practical advice. He or she will offer a suggestion. Use the topics and expressions in the boxes or your own ideas.**

A Uh, do you have a minute? I need your advice on something.
B Sure. What can I help you with?
A Some friends of mine are coming to town for the weekend, and I don't have any idea where to take them.
B I'd suggest going to the flea market.
A That's a good idea. I hadn't thought of that.

Some topics
where to take an out-of-town guest
what to wear somewhere
what to make for an important dinner
buying something
how to get information about something
how to get out of a commitment (something you've told someone you'd do)

Some ways to ask for advice
I need your advice.
Do you think I should . . . ?
Am I supposed to . . . ?
I can't decide if I should . . .
I don't have any idea . . .
If you were me, would you . . . ? (informal)

Some ways to give advice
I'd (I wouldn't) suggest . . .
Why don't you . . . ?
How about . . . ?
Have you tried . . . ?
You could . . .
If I were you, I'd . . .

The expressions *I'd suggest . . . , How about . . . ?* and *Have you tried . . . ?* are followed by gerunds.

2 ▶ **Listen to the conversation.**

A Speaking in front of people really makes me nervous.
B If you practiced more, you'd probably get used to it. I'd suggest signing up for a course in public speaking.

▶ **Complete the sentences below with gerunds (verb + *ing*). Then act out conversations similar to the conversation above. Your partner will give you advice on your problems.**

1. _____ makes me nervous.
2. _____ is something I find difficult.
3. _____ is something I've never enjoyed doing.
4. _____ is something I don't think I'll ever be able to do.

3 ▶ **Study the frame: Gerund vs. *it* as subject**

Subject		
Speaking in public	makes me nervous.	
It	makes me nervous	to speak in public.

4 ▶ **Rewrite the advertisement, changing the parts of the sentences in brackets [ ] as in the example.**

Making a good impression is important. It's our business . . .

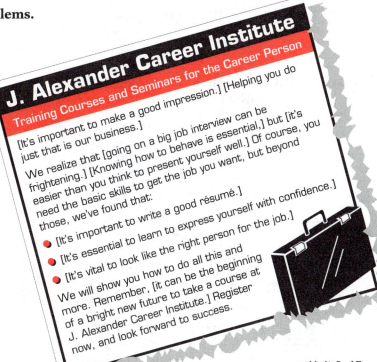

J. Alexander Career Institute
Training Courses and Seminars for the Career Person

[It's important to make a good impression.] [Helping you do just that is our business.]

We realize that [going on a big job interview can be frightening.] [Knowing how to behave is essential,] but [it's easier than you think to present yourself well.] Of course, you need the basic skills to get the job you want, but beyond those, we've found that:

• [It's important to write a good résumé.]
• [It's essential to learn to express yourself with confidence.]
• [It's vital to look like the right person for the job.]

We will show you how to do all this and more. Remember, [it can be the beginning of a bright new future to take a course at J. Alexander Career Institute.] Register now, and look forward to success.

TALK ABOUT CUSTOMS

5 ▶ **Using the information in the box or your own information, tell another student about a time when you did something culturally inappropriate.**

A It's so easy to offend people when you don't know their customs. I remember one time _____ . Later I found out _____ .

B _____ must have _____ .

Some customs
In Switzerland, it's considered impolite to take food with you to a dinner at someone's home.
In Japan, you should never leave your rice bowl on the table while you eat.
In Lebanon, you're not supposed to show that you're hungry when you go to someone's home for dinner.
In the United States, you should always ask your host before you take a friend along to dinner.

TALK ABOUT SOCIAL RULES

 6 ▶ **Listen to the conversation.**
▶ **Act out similar conversations with a partner. Discuss a rule of social behavior in your country, using the topics and expressions in the boxes.**

Use *must* to express a strong obligation and *mustn't* to express a strong prohibition.

A In my country, you must always give taxi drivers a tip. Tips are a big part of their salary.

B Really? What about maids in hotels? Do you have to tip them?

A Well, you're supposed to, unless the tip is included on your bill.

Some topics
giving and receiving tips, gifts, or compliments
arriving on time
invitations and table manners
shaking hands, kissing, bowing
use of first names and titles (Mr. Mrs., Ms., etc.)
special language to use with people of different ages and statuses

Some expressions
You must . . .
You mustn't . . .
You have to . . .
You don't have to . . .
You're not supposed to, but . . .
Do you have to . . . ?
Is it O.K. if . . . ?

 7 ▶ **Listen and match each conversation with the correct picture.**

MUST AND *MUSTN'T* FOR OBLIGATION AND PROHIBITION VS. LOGICAL CONCLUSION

8 ▶ **Study the frames: *Must* and *mustn't*: for obligation and prohibition vs. logical conclusion.**

Affirmative statements		
I You	**must**	go now. be on time.

Negative statements		
We You	**mustn't**	be late for dinner. wear shoes in the house.

must not → mustn't

Must vs. *have to*	

Use *must* to express a strong obligation.
  I *must* finish the report tomorrow. (It's extremely important.)
	Also use *have to* to express a strong obligation, although it is a little less forceful than *must*.
	  I *have to* meet Jim at seven. (I don't want to be late.)

Use the negative of *must* to express a prohibition.
  We *mustn't* call Susan so early. (We might wake her up.)
	Use the negative of *have to* when there is no obligation.
	  We *don't have to* call Susan so early. (She'll be home later.)

Use *must* in official correspondence. We *must* receive your application by June 1.	

Must: obligation and prohibition vs. logical conclusion	
Obligation and prohibition	Logical conclusion

Use the contraction *mustn't*.
  We *mustn't* bother Joe. He's not feeling well.
	Do not use the contraction.
	  The restaurant is dark. It *must not* be open.

Use *had to* for the past form.
  I *had to* practice every evening for the concert.
	Use *must have* for the past form.
	  You played so well. You *must have* practiced a lot.

9 ▶ **Complete each sentence with an affirmative or negative form of *must* or *have to* and the verb in parentheses. Make sure to use the correct tense.**

1. We ___must___ (try) to talk quietly because *don't* Sarah is sleeping.
2. I _have to_ (leave) any later than five because Paulo is coming over at six.
3. Kay got home late because she _had to_ (take) the bus. Her car broke down.
4. You _must not_ (call) between eight and nine because I was home the rest of the evening.
   must have called

5. Dan _must not_ (remember) who I am because he hasn't said hello.
6. The Ramones _must have forgotten_ (forget) to meet us because they're always on time.
7. Charlie _had to_ (cancel) his trip to London because he couldn't get a passport in time. He was so disappointed.
8. I _didn't have to_ (work) late last night because I _had not_ finished all my work early.

9. Your turn

What advice would you give to each of the people in the pictures? Discuss each situation in groups.

🔊 Listen in

Read the statements below. Then listen to the conversation between Tim Cooper and Jane Molina, another teacher. Choose *a*, *b*, or *c*.

1. Tim's student Bobby Carlson
   a. doesn't ever bother his parents.
   b. is only four feet tall.
   c. gets sick often. ✔

2. Jane thinks Tim should
   a. take the boy to a doctor.
   b. get in touch with the boy's ✔ parents.
   c. talk to the principal.

Would you give different advice to Tim Cooper, based on his conversation with Jane? Discuss this question in groups.

Joan Chasen, a teenager from Chicago, is going to spend the summer in your city or country. She's never been there before, and she isn't very familiar with your customs.

Tim Cooper is a kindergarten teacher. One of the children in his class doesn't look healthy and often gets sick. Tim recently noticed that the little boy's lunch bag usually has only candy or cake in it.

Richard Diego just started a job at a large company. Richard used to have his own business, but he recently sold it. He's very independent and likes to make his own decisions. He's never worked in an office before.

Laurie Smith is having dinner with some friends of her parents, and everyone is discussing politics. Laurie strongly disagrees with the others' opinions and is becoming very angry as she listens to them.

Susan Chang is a chemist and she loves her job. The work is interesting and she's well paid. However, she's overworked because her boss doesn't work very hard. He takes long coffee breaks and reads the newspaper.

Mark Seda's cousin died on Friday. Mark has an important job interview the same day as the funeral. He didn't know his cousin well.

10. On your own

1. Write a letter to a friend of yours, asking for advice about a real problem you have.

2. Read the letters asking for advice. Then answer them.

Dear Ms. Abbott

Dear Ms. Abbott,

I can't seem to find a good job no matter how hard I try. I know I have good job skills, and I got good grades at school. But every time I leave an interview, I just know that I won't get the job. And sure enough, later the company calls me to say that they hired somebody else. What should I do?

"Frustrated and Unemployed"

Dear Ms. Abbott,

I'm very excited because a good friend of mine is getting married next month, and I've been invited to the wedding ceremony and the reception. The trouble is, I've never been to a wedding in this country before. I have no idea what to wear or how to act. For example, how should I greet the bride and the groom after the ceremony? And what about a gift?

"Excited but Nervous"

PREVIEW

FUNCTIONS/THEMES	LANGUAGE	FORMS
Persuade someone	Our course will help you get over your nervousness. We'll have you write speeches and then we'll let you try them out on your classmates. Most important, we'll make you realize that you *can* be an effective speaker.	*Have, make, let,* and *help*
Give an opinion Support an opinion	In my opinion, children need responsibility. If parents have children help with chores, the children will feel needed. What's more, they will learn to take care of themselves.	The definite article *the*

Preview the reading.

1. A status symbol is something a person has or displays so other people will think he or she is important. Look at the pictures and identify the status symbols. Do you know any people who have these status symbols? Would you want any of these items? Why or why not?

2. Before you read the article on page 22, look at the title and the illustrations on pages 22–23. Then work with a partner and discuss how the animals in the pictures might be status symbols.

11.

PETS AS

Status Symbols

by *Peter Muller*

Londoners who happened to walk along the Thames during the mid-thirteenth century might have seen a large white bear walking down to the river. Following behind would be a man, holding the bear with a long leash. The man would sit on the riverbank while the bear, still attached to the leash, would go into the water and fish for its dinner.

The bear belonged to King Henry III. Henry wanted to save money, so he had the bear catch its own food. The people of London must have appreciated his sense of economy since they paid for the bear's expenses.

Henry was not the first king to keep large pets. In fact, practically every royal head of state from the beginning of civilization to the French Revolution seemed to want to own animals of great beauty—animals that were the biggest, the strangest, or the most dangerous.

Both the ancient Egyptians and Chinese collected animals for pleasure. Chinese emperors kept them in places called "parks of intelligence," while Egyptian royalty kept monkeys, leopards, and occasionally a giraffe on the palace grounds.

Birds, exotic and familiar, were popular in Rome. When Octavian, later the Emperor Augustus, defeated Marc Antony in battle, he was supposedly given a raven trained to say *Ave, Caesar victor imperator*, "Hail, Caesar, victorious leader." Octavian was very pleased until he learned that the trainer had taught another raven to say *Ave, victor imperator Antoni*, in case Antony had won.

Snakes were so popular in Rome at one time that they became a nuisance in the city. Sometimes during banquets, they would glide over the tables and among the guests who were eating. Dangerous animals were tamed and then permitted to walk freely through the houses of the rich. The Emperor Elagabalus had lions and leopards that entered the dining room and even the bedrooms of guests.

As trade routes to Africa and Asia began to open up, every aristocrat wanted to have exotic animals. Louis IX of France had an elephant and a porcupine, Charles V of Spain had seven seals, and Henry IV of France had four monkeys and a parrot. Charles V of France loved birds and kept every room at Vincennes, where he grew up, filled with them. He put them in cages made of gold and silver.

Not only did rich people keep pets, **they** made **them** do strange things for **their** entertainment. Napoleon's wife Josephine had an orangutan that sat at **her** dinner table in a coat. A Portuguese princess went to the trouble of getting zebras because **she** thought **they** would look pretty pulling the royal children in a little carriage. To **her** great disappointment, **she** got no cooperation from the zebras.

Owning and displaying exotic pets has continued into more modern times. It is said that the French poet Baudelaire walked a lobster on a leash, and Jack Johnson, the American prizefighter, took his leopard for walks through the streets of Paris. But over the years, it has become obvious that the care of exotic animals requires specialized knowledge. Generally speaking, the feeling of both the public and the experts goes against keeping bears in the backyard or lions in the living room.

What a way to save money!

So glad you could join us tonight!

Ave, Caesar victor imperator!

Figure it out

1. **As you read, think about whether "Pets as Status Symbols" is a good title for the article. When you have finished reading, give reasons why or why not.**

2. **As you read the article, try to figure out what its main themes are. Then say *Theme* or *Supporting Fact* for each statement below. For each supporting fact, tell which theme(s) it supports.**

    1. Almost every king and queen until the French Revolution kept strange pets.
    2. Henry III had a bear that he used to take down to the Thames so it could fish for its food.
    3. The rich kept strange pets not only as status symbols but also for pleasure and entertainment.
    4. People still own exotic pets, but, in general, the public feels very differently about this now.
    5. Napoleon's wife Josephine had an orangutan that sat at her dinner table in a coat.

3. **Match each highlighted pronoun in the next to last paragraph with a word or expression it refers to. The pronouns are listed in the order in which they appear.**

1. they	a. the zebras
2. them	b. the pets
3. their	c. the rich people ('s)
4. her	d. the Portuguese princess ('s)
5. she	e. Josephine's
6. they	
7. her	
8. she	

4. **The suffix *-tion* changes a verb into a noun, as in *civilize* and *civilization*. Complete each sentence with the correct noun from the list.**

appreciation	graduation	revolution
civilization	permission	transportation
cooperation	reservation	

    1. When a Portuguese princess tried to have zebras pull her children in a carriage, she got no _____ from the zebras.
    2. The French _____ took place in 1789.
    3. I'm looking forward to my college _____ .
    4. At many restaurants you need a _____ for dinner.
    5. I helped a friend with a report, and she took me out to dinner to express her _____ .

12. Oh, come on, Dad!

1. Discuss the advantages and disadvantages of having house pets. What kinds of animals make good pets? What kind of home is best for pets? What are some of the reasons people get pets?

Ten-year-old David Mandel is trying to talk his parents into taking in a friend's dog.

Listen to the conversation.

2

Mrs. Mandel	I have something to ask you.
Mr. Mandel	I hope it's not about money.
Mrs. Mandel	No, not exactly. It's about David's friend Ted and his dog Charlie.
Mr. Mandel	What's the problem?
Mrs. Mandel	Well, Ted's leaving for camp in two weeks, and he still hasn't found anyone to take care of Charlie.
Mr. Mandel	That doesn't surprise me. The dog has a miserable personality.
Mrs. Mandel	So David was wondering . . .
David	Why can't Charlie stay here?
Mrs. Mandel	Stay here? I don't think Charlie is what we need right now. In any case, the landlord probably wouldn't let us keep him. He's afraid of dogs.
David	True, but Charlie's just a little dog.
Mr. Mandel	That's the worst kind. What's more, with our luck, the dog would bite him and he'd make us move out.
David	Please, I'll take care of him. It'll be fun.
Amy	I could help David walk him.
Mr. Mandel	Do you kids realize how much work a dog is?
Mrs. Mandel	You know, it might be good for them, Paul. It would teach them responsibility.
Mr. Mandel	I wonder about that. Besides, suppose they get tired of him after a week? Then what?
David	We won't, we promise! Oh, come on, Dad! Wouldn't it be nice to be greeted by Charlie, wagging his tail? Just think of the love and affection . . .
Mr. Mandel	I have a family for love and affection.
Mrs. Mandel	It *would* help Ted out. . . .
Mr. Mandel	Hmm, I can see I'm outnumbered. O.K., I give in, as long as no one makes me do anything.

3. Find at least three arguments in the conversation for keeping Charlie and three against keeping him.

4. Complete each sentence with *the* or nothing.

1. I don't want Charlie. _____ dog has a miserable personality.
2. Our landlord is afraid of _____ dogs.
3. You should give your children _____ responsibility.
4. Just think of _____ affection that Charlie would show us.
5. I get _____ affection from my family.
6. I think _____ pets are a lot of work.

13. I hadn't thought of that.

1 ▶ Find these expressions in the conversation on page 24, and notice how they are used. (All of them except *What if . . . ?* appear.)

Make another point	Suggest a possibility
Besides . . . What's more . . . In any case . . .	Suppose (that) . . . ? What if . . . ?

State a reservation	State a condition
True, but . . .	As long as . . .

Use a past form with *Suppose* . . . ? and *What if* . . . ? when the possibility is contrary-to-fact. Compare:
  Suppose Victor *is* at home? (He might be.)
  Suppose Victor *were* rich? (He's not.)

2 ▶ Work with a partner. Play these roles.

Student A You and Student B are going to spend a week with some friends who live in another city. The trip takes 10 hours by car. You want to drive the 10 hours in one day, but Student B would rather break the trip into two days. Persuade Student B to drive the trip in one day, using the arguments in the box. Use the expressions in exercise 1 to connect your ideas.

Some arguments for driving in one day

We'd get there sooner.
We'd have more time with our friends.
We wouldn't waste two whole days getting there.
We wouldn't have to spend money on a hotel.

Student B You and Student A are going to spend a week with some friends who live in another city. The trip takes 10 hours by car. You want to break the trip into two days, but Student A would rather drive the 10 hours in one day. Persuade Student A to break the trip into two days, using the arguments in the box. Use the expressions in exercise 1 to connect your ideas.

Some arguments for driving in two days

Getting there could be part of the fun.
We could take our time and enjoy the trip.
We could stay in an inexpensive place.
We'd get there more rested.

You may say:
  We *'d* get there sooner (if we drove there in one day).
  We *'ll* get there sooner (if we drive there in one day).

3 ▶ Listen to the conversation.
▶ Complete the sentences.
▶ Act out similar conversations with a partner. Try to persuade your partner to change his or her mind about each sentence. Then change roles.

A One thing I'll never buy is a car. As long as I live near town, I don't need one. Besides, I hate to drive. It makes me nervous.
B Yes, but maybe it makes you nervous because you're not used to it. Suppose you drove more? You might start to enjoy it.
A Hmm . . . that's a good point. I hadn't thought of that. . . .

1. One thing I'll never buy is _____ .
2. I can't understand why people spend their money on _____ .
3. One place I have no desire to visit is _____ .
4. _____ is something I have no interest in.

Some expressions

| Yes, but . . .
That's a good point. | Maybe you're right.
I'm still not convinced. |

4 ▶ Listen to the conversations and check (√) the appropriate column.

The first speaker was . . .

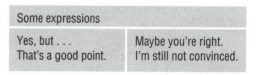

	persuaded	not persuaded
1.	___	✓
2.	✓	___
3.	✓	___
4.	___	✓

5 ▶ Your partner has trouble speaking in public. You once took the "Speak Effectively" course. Try to persuade your partner to take the course, too. Use the expressions in the box.

It helped me . . .
They had us . . .
They led us . . .
It made me . . .

SPEAK EFFECTIVELY

Do you get "butterflies" in your stomach whenever you have to speak in front of a group? Do you hate making speeches? Are you shy?

Our course will help you get over your nervousness and develop self-confidence. We'll have you write speeches and then, in a safe, supportive environment, we'll let you try them out on your classmates. Most important, we'll make you realize that you can be an effective speaker.

Sign up today. Write or call:

The Spring School of Speech

85 Chelsea St.   Los Angeles, California 90052   (213) 555-9835

6 ▶ Study the frame: *Have, make, let,* and *help*

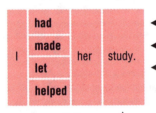

I	**had**	her	study.
	made		
	let		
	helped		

◀ I instructed her to study.
◀ I forced her to study.
◀ I allowed her to study.

let let let → base form

Make can also be used to mean *cause*.
   The course *made* me feel confident. = It *caused* me to feel confident.

Make is often used with adjectives to mean *cause*.
   John *made* me angry. = He *caused* me to be angry.

7 ▶ Rewrite the advertisement. Complete the sentences with *have, make, let,* or *help*. Some items have two possible answers.

GET INTO SHAPE AT THE *Body Factory!*

It's work, yes. Our instructors are tough, and they'll _____ you work harder than ever. But you'll have a good time, too. The time will fly and the work will seem like fun. Our instructors will _____ you do exercises that you'll actually enjoy.

One of our experts will work with you to design a diet just for your needs. We won't _____ you give up everything you like to eat, either. Most important, we'll _____ you stick to your diet and lose those unwanted pounds.

As a special introductory offer, we'll _____ you come in and try our program for one week at no cost!

For more information, write or call: The Body Factory, 24 Main St., St. Paul, Minnesota 55101, (314) 555-9820

GIVE AN OPINION • SUPPORT AN OPINION • THE DEFINITE ARTICLE *THE*

8 ► **Study the frames: The definite article *the***

He's afraid of	dogs. **the** dogs next door.	◄	count noun
I hate	coffee. **the** coffee at Ray's Coffee Shop.	◄	mass noun
Dogs need	love. **the** love of their owners.	◄	abstract noun
I studied	Chinese.	◄	language
I get along well with	Mexicans. **the** Chinese.	◄	people
I used to live in I have cousins in	Greece. **the** United States.	◄	country

When a count noun is the subject of a sentence, either a singular or plural noun may be used to make a generalization.
A dog is a lot of trouble.
Dogs are a lot of trouble.

Use *the* before the people of a country only when the word is not made plural by adding an *s*.
the Chinese   *the* French

Use *the* only before countries whose names are plural or contain *United, Union*, or *Republic*.
the Netherlands   *the* Dominican Republic

9 ► **Complete the phrases with *a(n)*, *the*, or nothing, and then finish the sentences. You may want to use some of the nouns in the box. Share your opinions with another student, who will either agree or disagree with them.**

1. When I was ＿＿ child, my parents never let me . . . . I (don't) think ＿＿ parents should let ＿＿ children . . . .
2. My father always made me . . . . I (don't) think ＿＿ parents should make ＿＿ child . . . .
3. In my opinion, ＿＿ children need . . . .
4. . . . is something ＿＿ child often does not get enough of.
5. . . . are ＿＿ qualities I value most in ＿＿ people.

Some abstract nouns			
love	freedom	generosity	courage
affection	discipline	ambition	tenderness
guidance	approval	intelligence	independence
responsibility	loyalty	honesty	patience

10 ► **Write a paragraph supporting one of the opinions you gave in exercise 9. Include at least three arguments in favor of your opinion.**

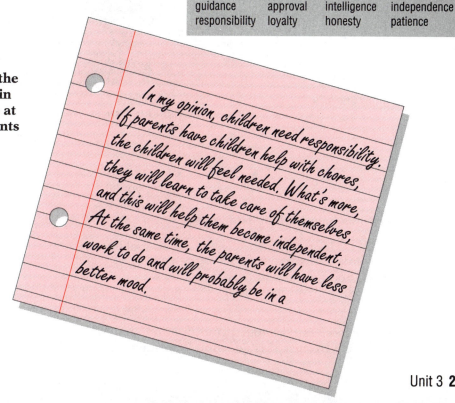

In my opinion, children need responsibility. If parents have children help with chores, the children will feel needed. What's more, they will learn to take care of themselves, and this will help them become independent. At the same time, the parents will have less work to do and will probably be in a better mood.

Unit 3 **27**

14. Your turn

There is a large vacant lot near your house, and the city is trying to decide how to use the land. You are at a community meeting, which was planned so you and others in the neighborhood could present your views. Look at the photos, which show the different possibilities under consideration for the land. What do you think your neighborhood needs most? Why? Work in groups and try to persuade the other people at the meeting of your opinion. Use the expressions "I (don't) think . . ." and "In my opinion . . . ." Be sure to state arguments in favor of your opinion.

the vacant lot

an apartment building

a castle

an office building

Listen in

Read the questions below. Then listen to the radio editorial and answer the questions.

1. What other words or expressions does Mr. Spector use to refer to teenagers?
2. What does Mr. Spector think the city should do with the lot?
3. What is one argument Mr. Spector gives to support his opinion?

Has the editorial you heard changed your opinion about the vacant lot in your neighborhood? Discuss this question in groups.

a community center

an art museum

a parking lot

a movie theater

a public garden

a hospital

15. On your own

1. Write one of the letters described below.

1. Write an answer to the editorial you heard in Listen In on page 29. Try to persuade Mr. Spector that the city should do something else with the vacant lot.
2. Write a letter to the appropriate official in your city, giving your opinion on the lot. Try to be persuasive by including as many arguments as you can to support your opinion.

2. Choose one of the following situations and write a note to persuade the person to change his or her mind.

1. A good friend of yours was planning to move to the city where you live. Suddenly, your friend has decided not to move after all.

2. You were planning to use the family car on Saturday to pick up two friends and take them fishing. Now your father says he has to wash and wax the car.

3. You and a friend were planning to take your vacations at the same time. You had planned to go to a beautiful Caribbean island together. Your friend just sent you a note saying "I'm not sure I want to go away on vacation. I have so much work to do."

PREVIEW

FUNCTIONS/THEMES	LANGUAGE	FORMS
Recall the past	When my brother and I were growing up, we used to spend summers with my grandparents in Brazil. Every morning we'd walk through the market place.	
Describe the past	When my grandfather was a boy, he lived on a farm.	The past habitual
Talk about how you've changed	I used to be very interested in philosophy. I never got tired of talking about the meaning of life. Now I don't have time to worry about such things.	Some verbs and expressions followed by prepositions

Preview the reading.

Student A   You are a land developer and would like to drain the swamp in the picture so your company can build a factory there. Try to convince Student B that your plan will help and not harm the community.

Student B   You are an environmentalist who wants to preserve the swamp and the surrounding area. Try to convince Student A to leave the area alone.

Everglades Evangelist

The meeting had been called to discuss the fate of a part of the Everglades, that grand swamp in south Florida known to the Seminole Indians as *Pa-hay-okee*, or "Grassy Water," through which the waters of Lake Okeechobee flow on their way to the Gulf of Mexico. Developers and farmers wanted to drain the water from a 240-square-mile area of the swamp and then use this land for luxury apartment buildings and farms. When conservationist Marjory Stoneman Douglas, then in her 80s, stood up to speak, her red straw "fighting hat" firmly in place, the crowd of farmers and developers

began to boo her. The slightly deaf Douglas laughed and said, "Boo louder." They did. She patiently waited until they had finished and then, as she had done so many times before, she spoke, calmly but with passion, of how the Everglades were a natural wonder that needed to be preserved.

Today, thanks largely to Douglas, that part of the Everglades remains unchanged. At the age of 101, Douglas spoke modestly of her achievement. "It had to be done, otherwise I wouldn't have done it," she said. "And I wouldn't have done it if I didn't enjoy it."

At the beginning of this century, the Everglades took up 9,000 square miles–an area more than seven times as large as the state of Rhode Island. It was filled with exotic animals like panthers and exotic plants like mangrove trees. "It was wonderful and beautiful and empty," says Douglas, who moved to Florida in 1915.

Born in Minnesota, Marjory was raised in Massachusetts by her mother and grandparents after her parents separated when she was 5. In 1913, a year after graduating from Wellesley College, she married Kenneth Douglas, who was 30 years older than she was—and who was soon in jail for writing a bad check. To speed a divorce, she moved to Miami, where her father, Frank Stoneman, had started the newspaper that is now the *Miami Herald*. When her father asked her to fill in for a reporter who was on leave, Douglas discovered the work she loved doing: writing. She worked on the newspaper for ten years. Then she quit, built a one-bedroom cottage where she still lives, and began writing for magazines. Her magazine work eventually led to a contract to research and write a book on the Everglades.

The Everglades: River of Grass was published in 1947, a time when the public was not yet aware of the effects that people have on their environment. Douglas wrote of how, because of human activities, "the Everglades were dying." She said the grass was dry and "brown as an enormous shadow where rain and lake water had once flowed. . .[so that] there was a sense of evil abroad, a restlessness, an anxiety that one passing rainfall could not change." The book forever changed people's view of the area, making them realize that it was not a dismal swamp, but a magnificent and very fragile environment that was home to many unusual animals and plants—an environment to be preserved, not destroyed. The book also marked the beginning of Douglas's fight to save the Everglades.

The year the book was published, the U.S. government made the Everglades a national park. But, ironically, government engineers soon began a series of projects that made Lake Okeechobee's waters go around, instead of through the park. Douglas was among those who opposed these projects. When a developer proposed making part of the swamp into a huge new airport in 1970, Douglas became a leader of the movement to save the Everglades.

Douglas formed a group, Friends of the Everglades, which helped block the airport and then kept up the fight by making sure lawmakers at both the national and state levels understood the importance of preserving the Everglades. The results were impressive. In 1984, the U.S. government decided that the lake's waters should again be made to go through the Everglades so that they could nourish the dry marshes. In 1991, Florida agreed to a system that would remove agricultural chemicals from the water that flows into the Everglades. In all, the national and state governments have committed $800 million to undo the damage they helped cause.

"That's all fine, but there's a lot more work to be done," says Douglas. She retired from the Friends of the Everglades to work on her eighth book. But, as she writes, her red straw fighting hat sits nearby—just in case her beloved River of Grass needs another helping hand from an old friend.

Marjory Stoneman Douglas

Figure it out

1. Read the article. Then complete these sentences.

1. A conservationist is someone who _____ _____
2. Marjory Stoneman Douglas's goal in life has been to _____
3. After moving to Miami, Ms. Douglas _____ _____
4. The Everglades: River of Grass is an important book because _____
5. The U.S. government became involved in the Everglades in the following ways: _____ _____

2. Find another way to say it.

1. Developers and farmers wanted to empty parts of the Everglades.
2. A crowd of farmers and developers made noises to show their disapproval.
3. Douglas spoke humbly of her accomplishments.
4. Marjory's father asked her to take the place of a reporter.
5. Douglas's book changed people's opinion about the Everglades.
6. The Everglades is a very delicate environment, home to rare kinds of wildlife.
7. The national and state governments have assigned $800 million to negate the damage they contributed to.

3. The suffix *-ness*, as in the word restlessness, can be used to change certain adjectives into nouns. Complete each sentence with an appropriate word from the list.

deafness	emptiness	redness
restlessness	dryness	impressiveness

1. The _____ of the results made the Friends of the Everglades happy.
2. Marjory Stoneman Douglas suffered from a slight case of _____ .
3. The nervousness of the farmers was like the _____ of the land developers.
4. The _____ of the grass made the Everglades look brown.
5. The _____ in the leaves of the trees showed they were dying.
6. Many unusual animals and plants once filled the space; now there was only _____ .

17. I remember ...

1. Tell another student about an older person you know or knew, such as one of your grandparents or great-grandparents.

 Bess Anderson is visiting her father, Charles Anderson, in Michigan. Bess's father is a widower.

Listen to the conversation.

2

Bess Hi, Dad. Mind if I join you?

Charles Not at all. Come and sit next to me.

Bess Dad, have you ever given any thought to moving south, to one of those retirement communities? It would be warm, you'd be with other people . . .

Charles I'm not interested in picking up and moving away.

Bess But don't you get tired of fighting the cold?

Charles Oh, I'm used to it. In fact, I've always liked the winter. I remember those cold winter nights when you and Jim were kids. We used to sit around the fireplace, the four of us. Outside the snow would be falling and the wind would be howling, but it was warm and cozy inside. I can still see your mother sitting in her rocking chair knitting.

Bess I always hated to get out of bed in the winter. The floor was so cold.

Charles And when you finally *did* get up, you were always so late you never had time to finish your breakfast.

Bess Well, I wasn't really that crazy about oatmeal.

Charles Off you and Jim would go, bundled up like two little Eskimos. Your mother would stand at the door and tell you to hurry or you'd miss the bus.

Bess We did once, you know. We were so afraid to tell you we decided to walk the five miles to school through the snow. Luckily, Mr. Fleming came along in his truck and gave us a ride.

Charles Hmm . . . There sure are a lot of memories in this house. . . . Well, I'd better be getting to bed. See you in the morning, dear.

Bess Good night, Dad. Sleep well.

3. Find these sentences in the conversation. Then say *present, future, one time in the past,* or *often in the past*.

1. We used to sit around the fireplace.
2. I'm used to it.
3. You'd be with other people.
4. Your mother would stand at the door.
5. Mr. Fleming came along in his truck.
6. You never had time to finish your breakfast.

18. When I was growing up ...

1 ► Listen to Alejandro describe a former time in his life.
  ► Work with a partner. Take turns describing former times in your lives, using the topics and expressions in the boxes.

When my brother and I were growing up, we used to spend summers with my grandparents in Brazil. Every morning, we'd walk through the market place on our way to the river. I remember so well all the different kinds of food for sale and the bright colors of the fabrics on display. At the waterfront, my brother and I would swim, and my grandfather would stand near the water with his pants legs rolled up and watch us. He wanted to make sure we didn't swim out too far. I can still hear him calling to us when we were only three meters or so from the edge, "O.K., that's far enough! Come back now!"

> **Some topics**
>
> a typical day or weekend when you were a child
> special occasion during your childhood, such as summers or holidays
> your student days
> your early married life

> **Some ways to begin**
>
> When I was growing up . . .
> During my childhood . . .
> Every summer . . .
> When I first got married . . .

> Use *used to* or *would* to talk about repeated activities in the past. If it is clear that the activity was repeated, you may also use the simple past.

> Notice how the present participle is used with sense verbs.
> I can still *see* my grandfather *standing* near the water.
> I can *hear* him *calling* to us.

A floating market in Manaus, Brazil, near the Amazon River.

2 ► Listen to Alejandro describe a specific experience in his past.
  ► Work with a partner. Take turns describing specific experiences in your pasts, using the expressions in the box.

A few years ago, I went back to Brazil. It was August, so many of the tourists had already gone home. I visited the familiar places—the waterfront, houses, cafés—the places where I had spent so many happy hours with family and friends. It was a quiet moment, a sweet one.

> **Some ways to begin**
>
> A few years ago, I . . .
> A remember one time I . . .
> Once I . . .
> Not long ago I . . .
> One day I . . .

> You can use the simple past, the past continuous, or the past perfect to set the scene for your story.
> It *was* August.
> It *was raining*.
> The tourists *had gone*.

> Use the simple past to tell what happened.
> I *went back* to Brazil.

3 ▶ **Study the frames: The past habitual**

Used to	Would	Simple past
Use *used to* talk about repeated activities. I *used to* go to the beach every day.	Use *would* to talk about repeated activities when you are continuing a discussion in the past. I *used* to spend a lot of time outdoors. I *'d* go to the beach every day.	Use the simple past to talk about a specific experience. Yesterday, I *went* to the beach (once). When a frequency expression shows that an activity was repeated, you may use the simple past. When I was a child, I *went* to the beach *every day*. Use the simple past after *when, before,* and *after*. When I *came* home from school, I'd do my chores.
Use *used to* with verbs such as *have, live, want,* and *like,* which express continuity but do not refer to repeated activities. I *used to live* in Rio. I *used to like* to swim.	Use *would* only with verbs that refer to repeated activities. When used with other verbs, *would* has a conditional meaning. I'*d live* in Rio (if I could).	Use the simple past when it is clear that you are expressing continuity. I *lived* in Rio for six years. I *never liked* to swim.

4 ▶ Rewrite the beginning of this chapter, completing it by using the verbs in parentheses appropriately. In some cases, you may use *would, used to,* or the simple past. In other cases, only one or two of these are appropriate.

Chapter One

When my grandfather ____ (be) a boy, he ____ (live) on a farm. He ____ (get up) at four in the morning to do his chores. First he ____ (milk) the cows and then he ____ (feed) the chickens. Sometimes he ____ (chop) the wood. After he ____ (finish) his chores, he ____ (walk) seven miles to school.

My grandfather never ____ (like) to get up early. From the time he was fourteen, he only ____ (think) of one thing—the city. As soon as he ____ (reach) his eighteenth birthday, he ____ (leave) the farm and ____ (get) a job in a factory. That's where he ____ (meet) my grandmother. The two of them ____ (walk) home together every day after work.

RECALL THE PAST

5
- ▶ **Look at exercises 1 and 2 on page 35 again and reread the stories told by the person from Brazil.**
- ▶ **Write your own story, recalling a time in your life and a specific experience from that time. In the first paragraph, give a general description (as you did in exercise 1). In the second, describe a specific event (as you did in exercise 2).**
- ▶ **Read your stories to the class.**

TALK ABOUT HOW YOU'VE CHANGED • SOME VERBS AND EXPRESSIONS FOLLOWED BY PREPOSITIONS

6
- ▶ **Study the frames: Some verbs and expressions followed by prepositions**

I dream I think I worry I often talk I'm nervous I'm excited	about	moving to Europe. going to Italy. saving money. leaving home. taking a trip. going away.
I'm interested I believe	in	teaching Spanish. helping people.

I'm afraid I'm tired I'm proud I'm jealous	of	living alone. being a student. having a good job. people who travel.
I'm satisfied	with	earning a small salary.

All of these expressions can be followed by nouns, as well as gerunds.
  I often dream *about my grandfather*.
  I'm proud *of my children*.

The word *get* may be used with some of the expressions above to mean *become*.
  I *got tired of* waiting, so I went home.
  I'm *getting nervous about* our exam tomorrow.

7
- ▶ **Listen to the speakers. Choose the sentence that responds to each speaker and complete it with the correct preposition.**

___ Thanks, I'm really proud ____ myself.
_1_ Yes, I am. I'm really interested _in_ learning Spanish.
___ Why should I? I'm satisfied ____ what I'm making.
___ Yeah, I'm really excited ____ going away.
___ No, he doesn't. He told me he's jealous ____ people who travel a lot.

8
- ▶ **Listen to the conversation.**
- ▶ **Act out similar conversations with a partner, using some of the expressions from exercise 6. Discuss how you've changed over the years.**

A I used to be very interested in philosophy. It fascinated me, and I never got tired of talking about the meaning of life. Now I don't have time to worry about such things. I'm more interested in practical problems.

B I've become more practical, too. I never used to think about my career. I would take odd jobs when I needed money. I believed in having a good time, and I never worked very hard. Now I think about the future a lot more. . . .

19. Your turn

Interview someone who is elderly or several years older than you. Find out what life was like when he or she was young. You may choose to interview a relative, a neighbor, a friend, or anyone else you know. Make sure to take notes so you don't forget the details. Then share the story with a group of classmates. Here are some questions to ask during your interview:

1. What different TV or radio programs were popular when you were young?
2. How were young people different? What did they talk and think about most?
3. What was a typical day like when you were a child?
4. What are your most vivid memories of your childhood? Could you tell me about some of your experiences?
5. What did your parents do? How were working conditions different from the way they are today?
6. How is life easier today? Can you think of some ways that it's harder?
7. What is the one way in which life has changed most over the years? Has it changed for the better or the worse?

roller skates

a plow

🔊 Listen in

Edna Olden, a sixty-five-year-old woman, is describing her mother's life as a young woman. Read the questions below. Then listen to Edna Olden talk about her mother and answer the questions.

1. What did she want most when she was young?
2. What kind of work did she do?
3. What did she have to do when she came home?
4. What was the Oldens' apartment like?

a box camera

an oil-burning lamp

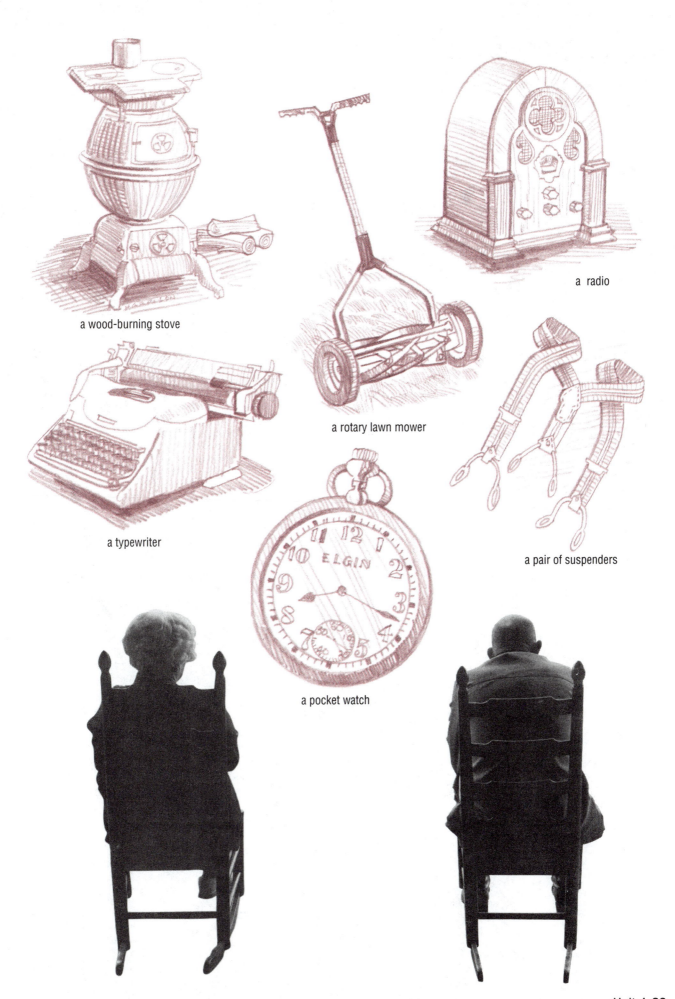

a wood-burning stove

a radio

a rotary lawn mower

a typewriter

a pair of suspenders

ELGIN

a pocket watch

20. On your own

1. **Write a short article, choosing one of the topics below.**

    1. Your local newspaper has asked you to write about the person you interviewed. Describe his or her past, using the information from your interview.
    2. You think life was easier (or harder) when you were a child. Support your argument by describing your childhood.

2. **Read the story. Then write your own description or story of your most vivid memory from the past.**

My Most Vivid Memory

I grew up on a farm in Minnesota, and I used to take long walks. One winter when I was about ten years old, I decided to walk to a river about three miles from our house. I wanted to see if the river had frozen. It was snowing lightly as I set out. I stayed at the river only a short time because when I got there, it had begun to snow heavily. I started walking back home very fast because the snow was getting thicker and heavier. Soon it was snowing so heavily that I couldn't see anything ahead of me except the footprints I had made on my way to the river. I kept hoping I would soon see the lights from our house. Then I noticed my footprints were gone; they'd been covered up completely by the falling snow! I was lost. I wasn't even sure which direction I should go in. I thought I would freeze to death and die in the snow. Then, all of a sudden, I heard a faint barking sound. It was our neighbor's dog, Sparky. Sparky found me and led me back to our neighbor's farm house. I was safe at last.

PREVIEW

FUNCTIONS/THEMES	LANGUAGE	FORMS
React to an event or a story	What a strange experience that must have been! How incredible!	*How . . . !* vs. *What a . . . !*
Tell a story	A toymaker climbed the World Trade Center yesterday. He'd never climbed it before. He was climbing the tower when the police arrived. I saw the water rising. I heard my friend scream.	The simple past vs. the past perfect vs. the past continuous Sense verbs with base and progressive forms of verbs

Preview the reading.

1. Have you ever tried mountain climbing or a sport or activity that involved a lot of risk or danger? Tell a partner about your experiences.

2. Before you read the article on pages 42–43, look at the title and the illustrations. What do you think the article is about?

HANGING TOUGH

They are the sort of friends who are so close they trust each other with their lives.

If one falls, the other is there to catch him. If one needs a lift over some obstacle that seems impossible to get beyond, the other won't leave until the obstacle is conquered.

They are Mark Wellman, 31, the Yosemite National Park ranger whose paralyzed legs don't keep him from rock climbing, and Mike Corbett, 37, a medical clinic janitor and the most experienced rock climber in Yosemite.

Their friendship served each of them well over the two brutal weeks they struggled up Half Dome, climbing hand over hand up the famous Yosemite 2,000-foot rock formation. When the pair reached the top, they were met by Wellman's girlfriend and an admiring crowd of news reporters.

Using skill and strength, Corbett led the way up one of the most difficult routes on Half Dome. And Wellman was there for his able-bodied friend early in the climb when pieces of rock gave way, 700 feet above the group, and Corbett plunged downward. Wellman locked their rope in place, stopping the fall at 20 feet. When it was all over, both men spoke as if there hadn't been a serious problem, but by acting quickly, Wellman probably saved his friend's life.

"Your partner can save your life—you can save your partner's life," Wellman said as the pair received congratulations from friends. "There are real close bonds."

Wellman and Corbett have now climbed together many times. On their climbs, Corbett must take the lead and, in effect, climb the rock twice. He pounds in the metal spikes that guide the ropes and climbs up. Then, after Wellman pulls himself up the rope, Corbett backtracks to remove the spikes and climbs up again. On Half Dome this process was repeated, time and again, inch by inch, for 13 days.

As evidenced by his arm and chest muscles, Wellman's job is not easy either. Wellman gets himself up the rope through upper body strength alone. In all, Wellman figures that on the climb up Half Dome he did 5,000 pullups up the rope, each time gaining no more than six inches.

When the two men first met, they never talked about climbing. "He knew that was how I got hurt—he didn't want to upset me," Wellman said. He was 22 when he slipped while climbing and fell 50 feet. That fall paralyzed his legs.

Then one day Wellman showed his friend a copy of Sport 'N Spoke, a magazine for disabled athletes. On the cover was a photo of a woman in a wheelchair being lowered down a rock. Corbett asked Wellman if he wanted to climb again.

That same night they made plans, and the next morning, ropes in hand, they met to begin training. Within six months, they had climbed El Capitan, the rock formation that dominates the right side of Yosemite Valley. And now they have climbed Half Dome, up a route so dangerous because of its crumbly granite that fewer than 30 people have climbed it.

Wellman said he is not trying to send any message to disabled people by climbing.

"Everyone has their own goals," Wellman said. "I don't climb rocks to say that this is what a disabled person can do." He simply hopes people

will see that he climbed before his accident and is still climbing after it—"No big deal."

Corbett wants to bring attention to climbing, his first love, and hopes someone somewhere will find inspiration. "I encourage other able-bodied people to stop and make a friend," Corbett said. "Never underestimate a person with a disability. They can blow your mind."

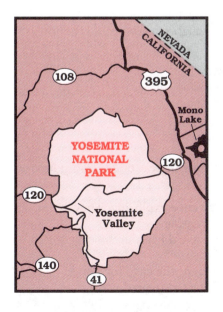

Figure it out

1. Read the questions. Then read the article and answer the questions.

1. How did Mark Wellman and Mike Corbett become friends?
2. Why did Mark Wellman climb Half Dome?

2. Read the questions. Then scan the article to find the answers.

1. How old were the climbers when this article was written?
2. Was anyone waiting for them when they reached the top of Half Dome? Who?
3. What happened to Mark Wellman when he was 22 years old?
4. How long did it take Wellman and Corbett to climb Half Dome?

3. Choose *a* or *b*. Find the sentences in the article that support your answers.

1. a. It was Mike Corbett who first brought up the idea of Mark Wellman's climbing again.
   b. Wellman showed Corbett a magazine about climbing and thensuggested they climb together.

2. a. Corbett and Wellman climbed Half Dome before trying El Capitan.
   b. Corbett and Wellman climbed was El Capitan before Half Dome

3. a. Corbett probably saved Wellman's life when Wellman fell during their climb up Half Dome.
   b. Wellman probably saved Corbett's life when Corbett fell during their climb up Half Dome.

4. a. Through his climbing, Wellman is not trying to send any messages to other disabled people; he simply wants people to see that he can climb again.
   b. Wellman says that he hopes his climbing will help show other disabled people how to reach their goals.

4. The prefix *dis-* may be placed before certain nouns like *ability* to indicate the "absence of something." Using your dictionary if necessary, complete each of the sentences below with one of the words from the list.

disadvantage   disbelief   disability   disagreement

1. Just because a person has a _____ doesn't mean that person cannot overcome many obstacles.
2. One _____ of wearing a helmet is the extra weight it places on your head.
3. What a _____ they just had! They never seem to see eye-to-eye on anything.
4. The judge in traffic court expressed his _____ over the excuse I gave her for speeding.

22. Did I ever tell you...?

1. Have you ever had an exciting adventure or a very frightening experience? Tell another student about it. Start like this:

Did I ever tell you about the time . . .

Anne Christopher is telling her friends Steven Wong and Maria Diaz about a frightening experience she once had.

Listen to the conversation.

2

Anne   Did I ever tell you about the time I almost drowned in a cave?

Maria   No! How horrible! What were you doing in a cave?

Anne   Tom Riley and I used to go cave exploring a lot.

Steven   Oh, wait. . . . I think I've heard this story. Didn't you go into a cave when it was raining?

Anne   Well, it wasn't raining when we went in. In fact, they'd predicted good weather the day before. The rain just came out of nowhere once we'd been in the cave for an hour or so. And water started rushing in.

Maria   You must have been terrified.

Anne   Well, I wasn't exactly thrilled. Especially when I looked down and saw the water level rising fast.

Maria   What did you do?

Anne   Tom and I separated and climbed up onto the highest places we could find. Of course, it was dark except for our flashlights. All of a sudden, I heard Tom scream.

Steven   Oh, yeah, a bat swooped down in his face, right?

Maria   I would have died.

Anne   Believe me, it was a close call. Fortunately, it didn't rain long, but we still had to wait there for hours for the water level to go down. And the bat was flying around the whole time.

Maria   What a frightening experience that must have been!

Anne   Well, looking back on it, it seems exciting. But I must admit I was pretty scared at the time.

3. Choose *a* or *b* for each sentence.

a. The sentence describes an event.
b. The sentence describes a continuous action or situation.

1. Tom screamed.
2. The water was rising.
3. A bat swooped down.
4. It wasn't raining.

4. Combine each pair of sentences using *before* or *after*.

1. We decided to go cave exploring. They'd predicted good weather.
2. It started to rain. We'd been in the cave for about an hour.
3. We'd already been in the cave for hours. The water level started to go down.

23. How horrible! How did it happen?

1 ▶ **Listen to the conversation.**

A Did I ever tell you about the time I went cave exploring and almost drowned?

B No! How horrible! How did it happen?

▶ **Complete the sentences with the verbs in parentheses, using the simple past or the past continuous. Then act out conversations similar to the conversation above. Your partner will react appropriately, using the reactions in the box.**

1. I _____ (go) cave exploring and almost _____ (drown).
2. I _____ (shop) in a department store, and Tom Cruise _____ (come in) to buy a tie.
3. A tree _____ (fall) on my car during a snowstorm and completely _____ (destroy) it.
4. I _____ (get up) to give a speech in front of two hundred people and _____ (notice) I _____ (wear) two different shoes.
5. I _____ (eat) dinner when a tarantula _____ (walk) across my plate.
6. I _____ (lose) a race because I _____ (fall down) just before the finish line.

Some reactions
How horrible!
What a frightening experience!
That must have been terrifying!
You must have been terrified!
I would have been very upset!
I would have died (panicked, fainted)!

Some present and past participles	
depressing	depressed
disappointing	disappointed
embarrassing	embarrassed
exciting	excited
frustrating	frustrated
terrifying	terrified

2 ▶ **Study the frames: *How...!* vs. *What a...!***

That must have been	frightening!
	a depressing feeling!

▶

How	frightening	(that must have been)!
What a	depressing feeling	

how + adjective or adverb
what a (+ adjective) + noun

3 ▶ **Listen to the conversation.**
▶ **Act out similar conversations with a partner. Tell your partner about a dangerous, funny, embarrassing, or disappointing experience you've had. Your partner will react, using adjectives and nouns from the box or others that are appropriate.**

A I hadn't seen my old friend Pablo in twenty years. He was my boyfriend in high school, but we never kept in touch. Then one day I ran into him in a movie theater.

B What a strange experience that must have been!

A It sure was! We found we have even more in common now. We're going out again.

B How incredible!

Some adjectives	Some nouns
embarrassing	situation
disappointing	story
funny	ending
strange	experience
incredible	problem
terrible	reaction
depressing	feeling

4 ► **Listen and match each conversation with the picture it describes.**

5 ► **Study the frames: The simple past vs. the past perfect vs. the past continuous**

Use the simple past to report an event in the past.
A toymaker *climbed* the World Trade Center yesterday.

Use the past perfect to report a situation or an event that ended before another point in the past.
He *'d* never *climbed* it before.

Use the past continuous to describe the situation at the time of an event in the past.
He *was climbing* the tower when the police arrived.

6 ► **Rewrite the articles, putting the verbs in parentheses into the simple past, the past perfect, or the past continuous.**

Skater Has Close Call

AMSTERDAM, The Netherlands— Champion skater Mary Van Dine ___ (skate) on a pond near her home last night when suddenly she ___ (hear) the ice crack. Before she could react, she already ___ (fall) through the ice. Fortunately, her skating partner, Hans Dekker, ___ (skate) about a hundred feet ahead of her when she ___ (fall). He ___ (hear) her cries, ___ (skate) back to her, and ___ (pull) her to safety.
Both Van Dine and Dekker ___ (skate) on the pond many times before without incident.

Man Climbs 110-Story Tower

NEW YORK, May 26—A 27-year-old toymaker from Queens ___ (climb) the South Tower of the World Trade Center yesterday morning. Thousands of delighted spectators ___ (watch) the three-and-a-half-half-hour event. The climber, George H. Willig, ___ (plan) the expedition for a year and ___ (test) his devices four or five times but never actually ___ (climb) the tower until yesterday.

7 ▶ **Study the frame: Sense verbs with base and progressive forms of verbs**

	saw	the water	**rising**.
I	**heard**	my friend	**scream**.
	felt	my heart	**pounding**.

Use the base form of the verb to describe a momentary or completed action.
Use the progressive form to describe a continuous action. Compare:
   I heard Tom *call* my name. "Anne!"
   I heard Tom *calling* my name. "Anne, Anne, Anne!"

8 ▶ **Continue rewriting the following account of a fire, using sense verbs as in exercise 7. Change as many sentences as you can.**

I was lying in bed taking a nap last week when all of a sudden . . .

Eyewitness Account!

   I was lying in bed taking a nap last week when all of a sudden someone in the hall yelled "Fire!" I got up quickly and opened my door. Smoke was pouring out of the apartment next door. The hall was getting warmer. Just then, the fire alarm went off. My heart was pounding as I raced down the stairs two at a time. Other people were running down the stairs ahead of me. When I got outside, I experienced a great sense of relief. A cool breeze was blowing across my face. A few minutes later, fire trucks pulled up in front of the building.

9 ▶ **Read the story about the hiker. Then write an ending.**
   ▶ **Choose one of the headlines below, or make up one of your own. Write a short article, using the expressions in the box to connect your ideas.**

Some headlines
Mountain Climber Stranded on Peak for Two Days
Women Gets "Surprise of her Life"
Brothers Reunited After 40 Years
"I Still Can't Believe It"
Couples Lives Out Lifelong Dream

when	just then	a few minutes later
as soon as	suddenly	finally
right after	all of a sudden	

Hiker Thought His End Had Come

John Cunningham, 42, returned home safely last night after two terrifying hours in Rosewood Park. Cunningham had spent a pleasant morning in the park without incident. His problems began when he decided to leave the hiking trail and look around on his own. "I was just walking along," Cunningham told reporters, "when all of a sudden I heard someone scream. Just then . . ."

24. Your turn

The people in the pictures have all been in the news because of their exciting and sometimes dangerous activities. Look at the pictures and the captions. Then, working in groups, discuss the details of the events. Consider each of the following.

1. Tell the story of the event from the beginning to the end.
2. What did the person in the photo tell reporters? What reasons did he or she give for choosing this activity?
3. Were people watching? What were their reactions and opinions?
4. What happened to the person in the photo after the event?

🔈 Listen in

Read the statements below. Then listen to the conversation and say *Right* or *Wrong*. Correct the wrong statements.

1. Two summers ago, the man had a job near the place where Ellen Ross walked across a tightrope.
2. One morning the man saw Ellen walking across a tightrope between two tall buildings.
3. The police cheered Ellen after the event and didn't arrest her.
4. According to Ellen, she walked across the tightrope because she wanted fame and money.

Have you ever done anything really dangerous just for the excitement of it? Tell a group of students about your experience.

Daredevil Ellen Ross walking a tightrope between two skyscrapers in downtown Dallas

Carlos Costa taking another of his famous dives into the Pacific Ocean off the coast of Mexico

Max Hogan tempting fate at a recent circus performance in Minneapolis

"Magic" Myrna testing the "flying speed" of her favorite racing car at a recent stunt show in Alabama

The great alligator wrestler Jimmy Oseola performing during a recent show in Miami

25. On your own

1. Write a short news story, choosing one of the topics below.

1. You are a reporter who witnessed one of the activities in the pictures on pages 48–49. Write an account of the event. Make sure to include a headline for your story.
2. A local magazine has heard about the experience you described to your group on page 48 and has asked you to write a story about it. Your story must be 400 words or less. Include a suggested headline.

2. Look at the picture as you listen to the man's story. Listen again and summarize the story.

P R E V I E W

FUNCTIONS/THEMES	LANGUAGE	FORMS
Ask for and give an explanation	How come you stopped taking English? Well, I'd really like to continue taking it, but I'm too busy this month, so I think I'll wait until next semester.	Conjunctions *so, because, since, even though, although,* and *though*
Give reasons	Since it's such a beautiful day, why don't we do something outdoors?	
Talk about hopes and wishes	I hope Joan isn't sick. I wish Joan weren't sick. I hope my boss will give me a raise. I wish my boss would give me a raise.	*Hope* vs. *wish* in present and future time

Preview the reading.

1. Look at the pictures below and discuss them in groups. What is unusual about them?

2. A prodigy is a child with unusual ability. Before you read the entire article on pages 52–53, read only the first and last paragraphs. Try to figure out what a prodigy might say. Then say *Right* or *Wrong* for each statement below.

   1. I have already done a lot, and there's nothing much left for me to do.
   2. My classmates don't like me.
   3. I never feel alone.
   4. My parents are younger than most of my friends' parents.
   5. I often laugh about things that aren't funny to other children.
   6. I want to be just like everyone else.
   7. My parents don't encourage me to succeed.
   8. I've never made any money.

26.

The Mysterious Gift of the Prodigy

by Roderick Macleish

Wolfgang Amadeus Mozart will be remembered as one of history's most famous child prodigies. By the age of eight, he had performed in half the great cities of Europe and was about to write his first three symphonies. He died shortly before his 36th birthday. but the world recognizes him as one of the finest composers who ever lived.

For centuries, people have been amazed by children of unusual talent. Pianist and composer Felix Mendelssohn had composed a fair amount of music by the time he was 11. His fourth opera was produced in Berlin when he was only 18. John Stuart Mill, the nineteenth century British philosopher, read Greek at three and had worked his way through elementary geometry and algebra and a large body of literature and history by the time he was 12.

Success has not always brought happiness to prodigies. When he was 20, John Stuart Mill suffered a serious mental crisis. "I seemed to have nothing left to live for," he wrote years later. Other well-known prodigies have had similar experiences.

A number of history's most famous prodigies had something else in common: They did not live very long lives. Composer Franz Schubert died at 31. Scientist Blaise Pascal died before he was 40.

Even though there has been a fascination with child

prodigies for centuries, there has been little serious study of them until recently. Some surprising common characteristics have been identified. The vast majority are boys. They are usually first-born children of middle-class families. Often, their parents are past the usual child-bearing age. Many are born by Caesarean section rather than by natural childbirth. They often have parents who seem to be trying to realize their own ambitions through their amazing children.

Those who have studied today's prodigies closely have observed that they often live under the great weight of their loneliness. In school with children their own age they may become bored or frustrated, and simply turn off learning completely

Many children, as they enter adolescence, begin to turn to other teenagers for affection, encouragement, and a sense of belonging. This can be a very difficult time in the lives of prodigies. They know they're different, and other teenagers know it, too.

Not all prodigies, however, fit this pattern. Wang Yani, a Chinese girl, is a painter of magical talent whose pictures of animals and landscapes are full of life and complex emotion. Yani began painting at the age of 2 1/2 and had her first exhibition, in Shanghai, when she was 4. By the time she was 6, she had done over 4,000

Wang Yani began painting when she was 2. Here, at 14, she demonstrates her work at an art museum.

Wang Yani, a Chinese prodigy, painted Last Night I Dreamt I Saw the Racing Egrets when she was 11. The inscription says "Weaving in a pattern of black and white, the egrets moved in a great hurry. Last night's vision was still vivid in my mind, so I painted this. . . ."

paintings and had exhibitions around the world. But her brilliance and fame have not kept her from having many friends and growing up as a normal child in a small town in China.

Although a child may be born with outstanding genetic potential, this potential will not necessarily develop. "Just having the gene is not enough," says Harvard University psychologist Howard Gardener. Something in the environment must nourish the potential. In Yani 's case, that something is probably her father, who gave up his own career as a painter in order to nurture Yani's talent and growth.

And although many prodigies enjoy the satisfaction of extraordinary achievement, public praise, and material wealth, even the most successful sometimes question the value of their lives and accomplishments. "I have a longing which grows stronger as I get older," confesses the acclaimed American concert pianist Eugene Istomin, "to be mediocre." ▲

Figure it out

1. **Read the article. When you have finished, check your answers to the questions on page 51.**

2. **Which of these topics does the article discuss? Say *Yes* or *No*. If you answer is *Yes*, support it with at least one fact from the article.**

   1. the short lives of some famous prodigies
   2. the emotional problems of prodigies
   3. some famous women prodigies
   4. the personal life of Mozart
   5. some characteristics that prodigies have in common with each other

3. **Many adjectives can be changed into nouns by adding the suffix *-ness*. Complete the paragraph with appropriate nouns from the list. There is more than one possible way to complete it.**

   closeness   happiness   sadness
   friendliness   lonliness   strangeness

   Ruby was a child prodigy. She remembers the _____ she felt as a teenager when she had no friends. Ruby had talent and money, but she couldn't find _____ . Her parents thought they could see the _____ in her eyes.

27. Sometimes I wish . . .

1. Is there something in your life you're trying to make a decision about, such as choosing a field of study or a career, changing jobs, finding a place to live, getting married, or maybe just buying something? Tell another student about it and explain why you're undecided.

John Walsh is tutoring Luke Bennett in math.

Listen to the conversation.

2

Luke Gee, thanks for helping me, John.

John No problem.

Luke I just hope I pass the test on Monday. Let's face it, John, I'm no genius like you are.

John I wish you wouldn't call me a genius.

Luke Listen, any fifteen-year-old who's graduating from high school . . .

John I'm tired of everyone talking about it all the time, though.

Luke Oh, they're just jealous of you because you have no problems in school, so they try to make you feel really different from everyone.

John You know, you might find this hard to believe, but sometimes I wish I were worried about passing the math test like everyone else. I really envy you.

Luke Why would *you* envy *me*? Because I have trouble in math?

John Well, because you're on the soccer team, for instance . . .

Luke Listen, I just got an idea. Since we don't have to work on my math after the test on Monday, why don't we work on your soccer? You can come over to my house after school.

John I don't know, Luke. I'm terrible at soccer.

Luke That may be . . .

John How come you want me to come over then?

Luke Because I kind of like you, even though I'm jealous of you, too.

John (*Laughs*) You too, huh? Well . . . I guess so. I would like to play better.

Luke Great! Gee, I'd better get going. Thanks again for the help.

John Don't mention it. See you Monday.

3. Match.

1. How come	a. I do well in math.
2. Why	b. you want me to come over?
3. I hope	c. but they're jealous of you.
4. I wish	d. because he's got a lot of money.
5. You're smart	e. do you want me to come over?
6. You're lonely	f. I did better in math.
7. I envy him	g. so they're jealous of you.
8. I feel sorry for him	h. even though he's got a lot of money.

28. How come you stopped taking English?

1 ▶ **Listen to the conversation.**

A How come you to stopped taking English?
B Well, I'd really like to continue taking it, but I'm too busy
this month, so I think I'll wait until next semester.

How come . . . ? is informal.
Compare the formation of sentences with *How come . . . ?* and *Why . . . ?* How come *you don't* speak English? Why *don't you* speak English?

▶ **Complete the sentences. Work with a partner. Act out
similar conversations to the conversation above, beginning
with your completed sentences.**

1. I've decided to _____ .
2. I never learned to _____ .
3. I couldn't go to _____ .

4. I won't be able to _____ .
5. I've always wanted to _____ .

2 ▶ **Listen to the conversation.**
▶ **Act out similar conversations with a partner. Explain why
you like or dislike something, using *even though, although,*
or *though*. Use the topics in the box or your own ideas.**

A I hear you just moved into a new apartment.
B Yes. I'm really happy about it, even though I'm paying a much higher rent.

Some topics
your (new) apartment your (new) job a class you're taking the city or town you live in a certain sport or hobby

I'm really happy about my new apartment, even though I'm paying a much higher rent.

I'm a guidance counselor. Although my work is sometimes frustrating, I feel I can make a difference in people's lives.

I'm very happy with this English class. I don't have enough time to study, though.

3 ▶ **Listen to the conversation.**
▶ **Act out similar conversations with a partner, using the sentences below.**

A Since it's such a beautiful day, why don't we do something outdoors?
B That's a good idea. Maybe we could go for a walk on the beach. . . .

1. Since it's such a beautiful day, MAKE A SUGGESTION

2. Since you're not doing anything Friday, EXTEND AN INVITATION

3. TELL ABOUT A FUTURE PLAN, since I have the money and the time.

4. TELL ABOUT A PAST EVENT, since I had no money and no time.

5. Since _____ , PERSUADE SOMEONE TO DO SOMETHING

4 ► **Study the frames: Conjunctions** *so, because, since, even though, although,* **and** *though*

My new apartment is bigger,	**so**	I like it.
I like my new apartment	**because**	it's bigger.

◄ It's bigger. *As a result,* I like it.

◄ *The reason* I like it is that it's bigger.

Since	I like my new apartment, I'm willing to pay more.

◄ *Given the fact that* I like it, I'm willing to pay more.

I like my new apartment,	**even though**	the rent is higher.
	although	

◄ The rent is higher. *But I still* like it.

I like my new apartment.	The rent is higher,	**though**.

◄ I like it, *but* the rent is higher.

So and *though* are informal. *Although* is more formal than *even though* and is more often used in writing.

Because is used to give a reason. *Since* is often used to refer to a reason already given.
A John didn't study for the test.
B Well, *since* he didn't study, he probably won't do well.

5 ► **These letters will be better if more conjunctions are used. Rewrite the business letter on the left, using two different conjunctions presented in exercise 4. Rewrite the personal letter on right, using three different conjunctions.**

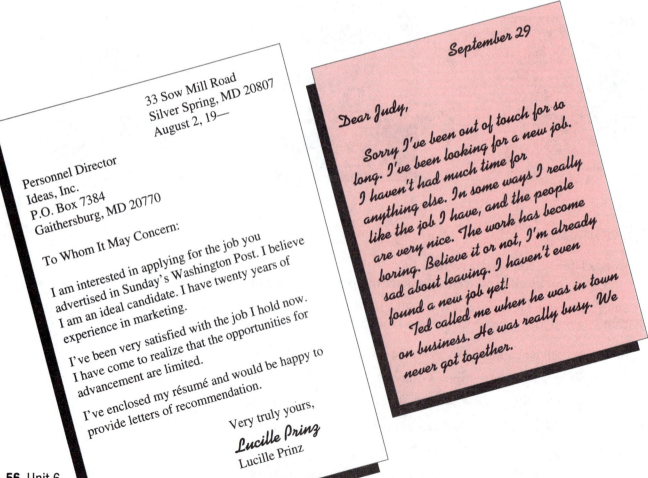

33 Sow Mill Road
Silver Spring, MD 20807
August 2, 19—

Personnel Director
Ideas, Inc.
P.O. Box 7384
Gaithersburg, MD 20770

To Whom It May Concern:

I am interested in applying for the job you advertised in Sunday's Washington Post. I believe I am an ideal candidate. I have twenty years of experience in marketing.

I've been very satisfied with the job I hold now. I have come to realize that the opportunities for advancement are limited.

I've enclosed my résumé and would be happy to provide letters of recommendation.

Very truly yours,

Lucille Prinz
Lucille Prinz

September 29

Dear Judy,

Sorry I've been out of touch for so long. I've been looking for a new job. I haven't had much time for anything else. In some ways I really like the job I have, and the people are very nice. The work has become boring. Believe it or not, I'm already sad about leaving. I haven't even found a new job yet!

Ted called me when he was in town on business. He was really busy. We never got together.

TALK ABOUT HOPES AND WISHES • *HOPE* VS. *WISH* IN PRESENT AND FUTURE TIME

6 ▶ **Listen to the people talk about their hopes and wishes. Match the pictures with the descriptions.**

7 ▶ **Study the frame:** *Hope* **vs.** *wish* **in present and future time**

Hopes and wishes about the present
I **hope** Joan **isn't** sick. (She might be.)
I **wish** Joan **weren't** sick. (She is.)

Use *hope* when you're talking about something that's possible.
Use *wish* when you're talking about something that's contrary-to-fact.

When it refers to the present or future, the verb following *wish* is a past tense form.
  I wish I *had* more time.
  I wish I *were going* to the party Saturday.

Hopes and wishes about the future
I **hope** I **can take** some time off next week. (I might be able to.)
I **wish** I **could take** some time off next week. (I can't.)
I **hope** my boss **will give** me a raise. (He or she might.)
I **wish** my boss **would give** me a raise. (He or she won't.)

When it refers to the future, the verb following *hope* is often in the present tense. Compare the meaning of these sentences.
  I hope I *pass* the test. (I haven't taken it yet.)
  I hope I *passed* the test. (I've taken it, but I haven't gotten the results.)

8 ▶ **Read about these people and say what they hope and wish.**

1. Bridget is worried about her son who's away at school. He hardly ever calls, and she can't get in touch with him.
   Bridget hopes _____ .
   She wishes _____ .

2. Anna is working against a deadline to finish a project. She doesn't think there are enough hours in the day to do the work, though.
   Anna hopes _____ .
   She wishes _____ .

3. Nina just moved to the United States and is looking for a job. Since she's not fluent in English, she's signed up for an English class.
   Nina hopes _____ .
   She wishes _____ .

4. Michael is an artist. He's worried about paying his rent this month because he can't make a living selling his paintings.
   Michael hopes _____ .
   He wishes _____ .

9 ▶ **Write a short paragraph about yourself that is similar to the items in exercise 8. End it with a hope and a wish.**

29. Your turn

Read about each family's situation. All of the couples mentioned have had to make decisions about the education of their children. What explanations can you give for why they made the choices they did? Do you agree with their their decisions?

🎧 Listen in

Luke and Kathy McNally are being interviewed on the radio program, *Educational Viewpoint*. Read the question below. Then listen to a short part of the program and choose *a, b,* or *c.*

Which of these sentences best summarizes the McNallys' point of view?

a. Skipping a grade won't make school interesting.
b. Teaching a child to be a good person is just as important as teaching him or her academic skills.
c. Children who skip grades are usually unhappy.

Work in groups to discuss the McNallys' decision. Do you agree or disagree? State your reasons.

Juan and Luisa Rosada's son, Rafael, was a concert pianist at the age of ten. He loved the piano and practiced at least five hours a day. Now Rafael is fourteen and he doesn't want to play anymore. The Rosadas do not seem upset and are not pushing him. Rafael was supposed to go to a private music school next year, but the Rosadas have now enrolled him in the local public school.

Lucy and Bob Clinton's daughter, Amy, is a child actress. Lucy Clinton started taking her daughter to auditions for TV commercials when she was three years old. Now Amy is ten and she spends almost all her free time in TV studios. Amy would rather stay home and play with her friends, but her parents don't want her to give up acting.

Lou and Sally Turner have two teenage children, Diane and Greg. Even though the Turners have the money, they want their children to pay for their own college education. Diane and Greg work three days a week after school in a local grocery store, baby-sit evenings and weekends, and have full-time summer jobs.

Nathan and Wendy Miller's children are also teenagers. The Millers do not want their children to work and are doing everything possible to pay for their education. The Millers do not have much money and have taken on extra jobs so that their children can go to college.

Luke and Kathy McNally have an eight-year-old son, Bobby. Bobby's teacher feels that Bobby learns more quickly than his classmates. The school has suggested moving Bobby to the next grade, but his parents have refused. Instead, the McNallys have convinced the school to let Bobby tutor a few of his classmates, and they are encouraging him to get more involved in after-school activities.

Marcy and Bill Wong have a nine-year-old daughter, Laura, whose situation was very similar to Bobby's. The Wongs had their daughter moved from the fourth to the fifth grade. Laura has had a little trouble making friends because she is at least a year younger than all of her classmates. She finds her schoolwork very challenging, though.

30. On your own

1. **Answer the letter. Tell your friend about your hopes and wishes for next semester or the future.**

2. **Write a personal or business letter, giving as many reasons as you can for any sort of decision you've made recently.**

Dear _____,

I'm really looking forward to next semester! There are so many things I want to do. I hope I can take fewer courses so I can get a part-time job. I also hope my parents will help me buy a car. I'm sure I'll need one if I get a part-time job. I also want to change some things in my life. For example, I wish I were in better shape. I really need to lose some weight. I hope I can find the time to go to the gym and exercise at least three times a week.

What about you? I know you're starting a new semester, too. What are your hopes and wishes? Write and let me know.

Love,

_____

Review of units 1-6

THOUGHTS WHILE FALLING 1,000 FEET TO THE SEA

MIDLAND, Mich.—As the airplane plunged 1,000 feet toward the icy water above the Arctic Circle, Ann Sinclair said she "just sat down and watched," silent, scared, and never expecting to live.

"The odds were about a million to one," she said. "We weren't supposed to live."

Miss Sinclair, 24 years old, a native of Midland, is visiting her parents this week after an oil company ship rescued her and five others from the water off northwestern Canada a week ago.

The twin-engine propeller plane crashed near Tukoyaktuk, above the Arctic Ocean, on Miss Sinclair's first assignment for the National Oceanic and Atmospheric Administration. Traveling with three other scientists, a pilot, and a copilot, she was sent to the area to observe Bowhead whales, an endangered species.

Their plane was 17 miles from its base at 1,000 feet when both engines died.

"It's funny, because . . . your instincts take over," she said. "I don't know what I was thinking. I never put on my seat belt. I just sat down and watched."

As the plane fell toward the water, survival suits were distributed.

"The pilot brought the plane down to 10 feet, then turned it into the wind so it stalled and dropped," Miss Sinclair said." The pilot was so good the impact wasn't as bad as it could have been, but it's like hitting a brick wall at 30 miles an hour. The only thing that saved us was the pilot's turning into the wind like that. He saved our lives."

Shortly before the crash, Miss Sinclair said she heard the pilot radio the position of the plane. After the plane hit the water, the passengers made their escape.

The process was slowed, however, when one of the scientists grabbed the handle of the emergency exit door and it came off in his hand. The crew and passengers finally got out through the front door of the plane, taking with them a life raft that had been placed on board only the night before.

Miss Sinclair said a lifelong bond has developed between her and the five others who went down.

"I'm so proud of this team," she said. "Everyone just moved. There was no room for emotion. No one panicked."

Miss Sinclair's agency has given her two weeks to recover from her experience, but she does not believe she will use it.

"I just think it's important to get back on the horse," she said.

---

1 ▸ **Read the article. Then put the events below in the correct order. Next rewrite the sentences in the past perfect.**

__ Terrified, Miss Sinclair watched the plane fall toward the icy water minutes before the crash.

__ Only seventeen miles from its base, the plane suddenly developed engine trouble.

__ The National Oceanic and Atmospheric Administration sent Miss Sinclair to the Arctic to study Bowhead whales.

__ Their plane crashed near the Arctic Circle.

2 ► **Put the verbs in parentheses into the simple past, the past continuous, or the past perfect.**

One fateful day in August, Ann Sinclair _____ (fly) over the Arctic Ocean. To Ann's horror, both engines of the plane suddenly _____ (fail) when the plane _____ (return) to its base. Fortunately, everyone _____ (escape) onto a life raft. After the plane _____ (fall) 1,000 feet and _____ (crash) into the icy water, the passengers and crew _____ (wait) for an hour on the raft. Finally, a ship _____ (rescue) Miss Sinclair and the five other people who _____ (be) aboard the plane.

3 ► **Rewrite this description of an earthquake, using the sense verbs *saw*, *heard*, and *felt*. Change as many sentences as you can, following the example.**

One evening I was at a party in a friend's apartment when I felt the walls and floor start to shake.

The Worst Experience of My Life

One evening I was at a party in a friend's apartment when the walls and floor started to shake. Things fell from the bookshelves and tables. Then someone screamed, "Earthquake!" My hands and face went cold. Someone passed out. The apartment was on the fourteenth floor of the building, and the hall was crowded with people. Someone was pushing me. A few people fell on the stairs. There was smoke drifting in the air, and the fire alarm went off. I was so relieved when the cold air touched my face!

4 ► **Bruce, who was at the party, is telling his friend Martha about the earthquake. Rewrite the sentences in brackets [ ], using *so* or *such* and result clause.**

Martha I read there was an earthquake while I was away. Was it bad?
Bruce [Yes, it was a very bad earthquake, and it destroyed several buildings.]
Martha Where were you when it happened?
Bruce I was at a party. I didn't get too nervous, but [one person was very frightened, and he fainted.] It seemed like hours before we got outside. [There were a lot of people, so we couldn't move very quickly.] When I finally got outside, [it was a great relief, and *I* almost fainted.]

5 ► **Read the statements below. Then listen to one side of a conversation about a hurricane. Each time you hear a pause, choose the appropriate response, *a* or *b*.**

1. a. What a frightening experience that must have been!
   b. How disappointing!

2. a. I would have panicked!
   b. How depressing!

3. a. How embarrassing!
   b. I would have been terrified!

Bickering Employees Are Bad News in the Office

by Beth Brophy

If you've ever spent time with a bickering couple, you can sympathize with managers who supervise two bickering employees.

"It's destructive if two people are arguing," said Marilyn Moats Kennedy, managing partner of Career Strategies in Wilmette, Illinois.

It hurts productivity, keeps the manager from other things, and often other employees spend time listening to it, so you're losing their time, too, Kennedy said.

As long as the problem employees have jobs that aren't related, separating them is the simplest solution, said Allan Cohen, management professor at Babson College and senior vice president of the consulting firm Goodmeasure Inc. in Boston.

But putting up fences won't work if job duties overlap. In that case, the manager must make them cooperate. "If two secretaries won't cooperate and answer each other's phones, I'll bang their heads together," Kennedy said.

Surprisingly, experts say the cause of the problem often lies within the company's structure.

"What looks like personality conflicts could be natural, based on organizational structure," Cohen said.

In a rivalry between sales and production managers, the salesperson might want many varieties of a product manufactured to satisfy customers; the production manager might want to manufacture one product to keep costs down. If two salespeople are fighting over customers, the organizational structure may encourage nasty competition, Cohen said.

Perhaps the employees who don't get along should report to separate people so they're not trying to get the same boss's time and attention, said Richard Miners, a partner at the management consulting firm of Goodrich & Sherwood in New York.

"Or maybe there's a communication problem, and only one person gets his or her words in and the other feels like a stepchild," Miners said.

The solution: The manager should make sure the company's reward system and division of jobs aren't creating the behavior problem.

"That's the case more often than personality," Cohen said.

Of course, sometimes there is a true personality conflict that the manager can't ignore.

In that case, "Bring both parties together and leave the room," said workplace psychologist Marilyn Machlowitz. "Don't attempt to mediate or you'll be the common enemy."

Warn both parties that if they don't begin to cooperate professionally, a lot is at stake, ranging from a transfer to unemployment. "Often one or both has to go," Machlowitz said, "because the work is not getting done. . . ."

6 ▶ **As you read the article, pay attention to the opinions in it. Then, when you have finished, say *Right* or *Wrong* for each statement below. Correct the wrong statements.**

1. Even if bickering employees share duties, the manager should separate them so they don't have to work near each other.
2. Bickering on the job is not always caused by personality conflicts.
3. If two employees with a personality conflict are bickering, the boss should be present to solve the problem.
4. It is natural for employees to bicker when the structure of the organization encourages competition.
5. If bickering employees don't have to share duties, sometimes a solution is to give them different bosses.

7 ▸ **These are some conversations taking place in an office. Combine the sentences in brackets, using** *so, because, since, even though, although,* **or** *though.* **Some items have more than one answer.**

1. **A** I've noticed the two of you haven't been getting along. [You may not always agree. You still have to work together.]
   B We know. We'll try our best to improve.

2. **A** Julia is never at work on time. [She's always late. She missed the important meeting yesterday.]
   B [You're going to have to talk to her. This really can't continue.]

3. **A** Two of my employees don't get along. Do you think I should talk to them?
   B I would if I were you. [They both work for you. Their problem is your problem, too.]

4. **A** I think you should consider firing Kevin Wells. He can't seem to get along with anyone.
   B [I know he's hurting productivity. I'd still like to keep him.] I think he has talent.

8 ▸ **Some employees at a company are talking about their bosses. Write a sentence summarizing what each person says, using** *too* **or** *not . . . enough* **with infinitives. Some items have more than one possible answer.**

1. YOSHI   My boss is really indecisive. He changes his mind about everything, so he never gets anything done.

2. MARIE   My boss is very busy. She says she wants to be helpful, but she never has the time to sit down and explain my responsibilities to me.

3. RENATA   My boss manages ten people, including me. She doesn't seem to know who is responsible for each project.

4. AHMED   My boss just came to our company. He's not very experienced, so he can't always give me the information I need.

9 ▸ **An office manager is talking to two problem employees. Complete what the manager says, using with a form of** *must* **or** *have to* **and the verb in parentheses. Make sure to use the correct tense. Some items have two answers.**

This bickering on the job _____ (continue).
Yesterday I _____ (stop) working twice to talk to you.
Everyone in this office _____ (waste) at least an hour because they were listening to you instead of working.
You both have good jobs here, but you _____ (want) to keep them. You _____ (settle) your differences right away. You _____ (agree) on everything, but you _____ (cooperate) with each other.

64 Review of units 1–6

HAITIAN IMMIGRANTS: AMERICA'S NEW SUCCESS STORY

When Berenice Belizaire moved from Haiti to New York City with her mother and sister, she was not very happy. She spoke no English. The family had to live in a tiny apartment. Her mother, a nurse, worked long hours. For the first time in her life, Berenice hated going to school. She had always been a good student, but now she was trying to learn a new language while putting up with insults and cruel jokes from the American students. Some students even cursed her in the cafeteria and threw food at her.

Two years later, at the beginning of her senior year in high school, Berenice was not only speaking fluent English but had also become one of the best students in her class. By the end of the year, Berenice was the valedictorian and she was chosen to be the student speaker at the school's graduation ceremony. Now Berenice is attending the Massachusetts Institute of Technology, one of the top schools in the country for science.

Berenice Belizaire's story is remarkable, but it is not unusual. New York City's schools have many immigrants who are proving to be outstanding students. The schools in New York are often crowded and lack money, so some people have argued that immigrant children, who may have special language needs, place too great a burden on the schools. They argue that immigration may be hurting New York.

According to some teachers in New York, this view of immigrant students is completely wrong. "The immigrant students are the reason that I love teaching in New York," says Judith Khan, an experienced teacher. "They have a desire to work hard and succeed that kids born in the United States no longer seem to have."

And what effect have immigrants had on New York? "Without them, New York would have been a smaller place, a poorer place, a lot less vital and exciting," says Professor Emanuel Tobier of New York University. Immigrants opened new stores and businesses, and they were willing to start by doing work that, while perhaps not very appealing, was extremely necessary.

The Haitians in New York have succeeded through hard work. Compared to all New Yorkers, a higher percentage of Haitians either have jobs or have started new businesses. In contrast, the percentage of Haitians who are poor is lower than average. As happened with immigrant groups before them, many Haitians have become "American success stories."

Of course, not all immigrants succeed. Some lose hope after years of working for little pay. Others, excited by new freedoms in the United States, lose their self-discipline. "I've noticed something that's very interesting," says Professor Philip Kasinitz of Williams College. "When immigrant kids criticize each other for getting lazy, they say, 'You're becoming American.' Ironically, the immigrants who are least influenced by American culture have the best chance of becoming American success stories."

If so, those who are worried about immigration have the problem backwards. The real question isn't whether the immigrants are hurting America, but whether America is hurting the immigrants.

---

10 ▶ **Read the article. Then complete the sentences with the definite article *the* where necessary. Next check (√) those statements which are main ideas from the article.**

1. ___ ____ story of Berenice Belizaire is remarkable, but not unusual.
2. ___ Berenice gave ____ valedictorian speech at ____ school's graduation.
3. ___ Through ____ hard work, Haitians have succeeded in ____ New York.
4. ___ Some immigrant children criticize each other for becoming ____ American.
5. ___ Like many immigrants before them, Haitians too can be called ____ examples of ____ "American success stories."
6. ___ Judith Khan is an experienced teacher in ____ New York school system.

---

11 ▶ **Andre Armand is a twelve-year-old Haitian refugee, and he's explaining how he learned to speak English so well. Complete the paragraph, using *let*, *make*, *have*, or *help*; a pronoun; and the verb in parentheses.**

I started school soon after I came here, and both my friends and my teacher *helped me learn* (learn) English. They were very patient with me and gave me confidence. There were several children from Haiti, but my teacher almost never _____ (speak) Haitian in class. He encouraged us to speak English, even though we made mistakes. He often _____ (work) in small groups with children who spoke no Haitian.

Sometimes I worried about ever graduating or becoming successful in life. My teacher _____ (understand) that concentrating on learning English was more important for now than worrying about being a big success.

My parents _____ (learn) English too, even though they knew very little English themselves. They _____ (study) every afternoon, and they only _____ (watch) TV after I had finished my homework.

12 ▶ **Gail Adams recently moved from the United States to Mexico to take a job. Complete the letter a friend wrote to her with forms of the verbs or expressions in the list and the correct prepositions. Some items have more than one possible answer.**

be afraid   be proud   dream
be excited   be satisfied   think
be jealous   be tired
be nervous   worry

Dear Gail,

Thanks for sending me the photo of the children in your neighborhood. It's hard to believe you've already been in Mexico for three months. I miss you a lot, and I _____ you almost every day.

I'm really happy that you _____ your new job. It sounds like a great opportunity. I admit I _____ you—it must be so exciting to live in Mexico.

Sometimes I _____ applying for a job overseas myself. I _____ living in California, and I'd like to try something really new and different, but I guess I _____ making a change.

Well, that's about it for now. Write when you get a chance.

Love,
Cindy

13 ▶ **Write a short paragraph comparing your life nowadays to your life when you were a child. Use *used to*, *would*, or the simple past in some of your sentences.**

When I was a child, I used to. . . .
Sometimes I would. . . . Nowadays. . . .

FOCUS ON THE EFFORT, NOT THE OUTCOME

by Marilyn Elias

Fourteen-year-old Richie Hawley had spent five years studying clarinet at the Community School of Performing Arts in Los Angeles when he was invited to try out for a concert solo with the New York Philharmonic.

Ninety-two young people were invited to the auditions; only nine won Lincoln Center solos. Hawley was among them.

The audition could have been the perfect setup for fear, worrying about mistakes, and trying to impress the judges. But Hawley says he "did pretty well at staying calm."

"And I couldn't be thinking about how many mistakes I'd make—it would distract me from playing," he says. "I don't even remember trying to impress people while I played. It's almost as if they weren't there. I just wanted to make music."

Hawley is a winner. But he didn't become a winner by concentrating on winning. He did it by concentrating on playing well.

"The important thing in the Olympic Games is not to win but to take part," said the founder of the modern Olympics, Pierre de Coubertin, 88 years ago. "The important thing in life is not the triumph but the struggle. The essential thing is not to have conquered but to have fought well."

Some people might think de Coubertin's words are naive, even self-defeating. But new research shows that his philosophy is exactly the path achievers take to win at life's challenging games.

A characteristic of high performers is their intense, pleasurable concentration on work, rather than on their competitors or future glory or money, says Dr. Charles Garfield, who has studied 1,500 achievers in business, science, sports, the arts, and professions.

"They're interested in winning, but they're most interested in self-development, testing their limits," says Garfield, president of Performance Sciences Institute in Berkeley, California, and a clinical professor at the University of California Medical School, San Francisco.

One of the most surprising things about top performers is how many losses they've had—and how much they've learned from each. "Not one of the 1,500 I studied defined losing as failing," Garfield says. "They kept calling their losses 'setbacks.'"

A healthy attitude toward setbacks is essential to winning, experts agree.

"The worst thing you can do if you've had a setback is to let yourself get stuck in a prolonged depression," says Milton Wolpin, a clinical psychologist at the University of Southern California.

Instead, Wolpin says you should analyze carefully what went wrong. Identify specific things you did right and give yourself credit for them, he says. He believes that most people don't give themselves enough praise. He even suggests keeping a diary of all the positive things you've done on the way to a goal.

Psychologist Lorraine Nadelman says parents should play games of both chance and skill with their children, and should emphasize the difference between the two.

Concentrating on the game instead of the outcome will also help you keep realistic expectations.

"A lot of people think if they win something big, it's going to make a drastic change in their lives," Wolpin says. "Then, if life settles down pretty much as before, it can leave you disappointed. Don't build up a lot of . . . unrealistic expectations."

---

14 ▶ **Read the article. Then mark the statements as follows: 1 = main idea; 2 = supporting detail; 0 = neither an idea nor a detail in this article.**

1. ___ Richie Hawley just wanted to make music.
2. ___ "The important thing in life is not the triumph but the struggle."
3. ___ Richie Hawley started studying at the Community School of Performing Arts when he was nine years old.
4. ___ High performers concentrate on their work rather than on their competitors or future glory or money.
5. ___ One of the surprising things about top performers is how much they learn from their losses.
6. ___ Parents should play games of both chance and skill with their children.

15 ▶ **Rewrite the paragraph, changing the parts in brackets, as in the example.**

Pierre de Coubertin, the founder of the modern Olympics, said that [it was more important to take part in something than to win.] Now experts agree that [thinking about the activity itself is essential] if you want to be a winner. Contrary to popular opinion, [competing isn't a good idea.] In sports, for example, [it doesn't help you win to compete against other athletes.] [Competing against your own record is better.]

[It isn't helpful to criticize yourself too much.] [It's much more important to concentrate on your successes.] [Writing down everything you've done right is a very good idea.]

Pierre de Coubetin the founder of the modern Olympics said that taking part in something was more important than winning. Now experts agree that it's . . .

16 ▶ **The members of a high-school soccer team are talking about a friendly game they're getting ready to play with another team during a community get-together. Complete the conversation with appropriate expressions from the box. Some items have two possible answers.**

Joe We have to win this game. We lost our last game. _____ we've never won a game with this team.
Kenny _____ this isn't a competition. We should just play for fun.
Joe I don't agree. _____ we're playing, we should play to win.
Paco I agree with Kenny. I think it's more important to have a good time. I mean, _____ we lose? What's going to happen?
Joe I really don't understand you two. When I play, I play to win. It adds excitement to the game.

besides	suppose (that)
what's more	what if
in any case	as long as
true, but	

17 ▶ **Read about these people. Then complete the statements appropriately.**

1. Last year Erica came in second in an all-day bicycle marathon. This year she's going to be in the marathon again.
   Erica hopes _____ .

2. Jon's basketball team is going to play an important game, but their best forward, Ned, has a sprained ankle.
   Jon and the rest of the team wish _____ .

3. Marina wants to be a research scientist, but her parents can't afford to send her to college. She's entered a competition for a scholarship.
   Marina hopes _____ .

4. Roberto's soccer team is going to have a game this afternoon. The game was supposed to be yesterday, but it rained all day.
   Roberto hopes _____ .

5. Christos is an actor, and there's going to be an important audition next Tuesday. They won't postpone the audition, even though Christos will be in Mexico on vacation next week.
   Christos wishes _____ .

6. Jenny likes to play team sports. The problem is she isn't very athletic.
   Jenny wishes _____ .

PREVIEW

FUNCTIONS/THEMES	LANGUAGE	FORMS
Make a complaint Make a forceful complaint	I'd like to know if my CD player has been repaired yet. It was supposed to have been ready last week. The parts have been ordered, but they haven't come in yet. Something must be done immediately!	The passive with present perfect verbs
State a problem	My car sounds like a motorboat at full speed. It looks as if you need a new muffler.	Sense verbs with *like, as if,* and *though*

Preview the reading.

1. Discuss with a partner the uses and advantages (or disadvantages) of the inventions shown below. Describe for your partner any other advances in technology you think might occur during the next century.

Welcome to the future!

2. Before you read the article on page 70, look at the title and the photos on page 71. Then work with a partner to discuss what the article is probably about.

31.

The LIGHT of the Twenty-first Century

A scientific discovery is often made long before someone is able to put it to use. For example, scientists discovered how to split atoms decades before the invention of the atomic bomb and the use of atomic power to produce electricity. But sometimes discovery and invention happen at the same time, as occurred more than thirty years ago with the discovery of coherent light and the invention of the laser.

The word *laser* stands for "light amplification by stimulated emission of radiation." To many people lasers are very mysterious, but a laser is simply a device that produces a very strong light. The light from a laser is called *coherent* light because it is light that moves in only one direction. In contrast, *incoherent* light, like the light from the sun or a light bulb, moves away from its source in all directions, so its strength is very spread out. The light from a laser, moving in only one direction and concentrated in a narrow beam, is much stronger.

Laser light is created by a process called *stimulated emission*. In this process, the atoms of a certain substance, such as a crystal or a gas, are excited in such a way that they produce coherent light. A person working with a laser can aim this coherent light, called a *laser beam,* in any direction.

As soon as the laser was developed, scientists began thinking of practical applications for it. One of the earliest uses was to make extremely precise measurements of distance and speed. For example, the distance to the moon was measured to within a foot, and the speed of light was measured to within a thousandth of a mile per second. As time passed, many more applications for the laser were developed.

Some of the most important uses of lasers are in medicine. Lasers can be used in surgery to open and close incisions with no danger of infection. In eye operations, a laser can be used to reattach a retina and to prevent excessive bleeding of tiny blood vessels in the eye. Lasers are also important in the treatment of cancer. A laser beam can completely destroy a cancerous growth without leaving behind any dangerous cancer cells that could start a new tumor. More recently, lasers have been used to remove skin discolorations like freckles, age spots, and birthmarks.

Some dentists have even started using lasers for painless treatment of teeth and gums.

A laser beam can be made narrow enough to focus on a single cell, on part of a cell, or even on individual atoms and molecules. In fact, lasers are now being used to "trap" atoms and slow them down, letting scientists study the ways atoms and molecules move during chemical reactions. This technique is being used in a variety of research projects—for example, to study how plants convert sunlight into energy through the process of photosynthesis, and to take a "snapshot" of the chemical reaction that is the first step in vision, when light hits the retina of the eye.

Over the past twenty years, personal computers have brought tremendous changes to the home and the workplace, and many of the most important developments in computer technology are based on lasers. From laser printers (including the newest color printers), to technology by which whole encyclopedias of information can be stored on a laser disk (called a CD-ROM) and read by a computer, to optical disks that have hundreds of times as much memory as regular floppy disks, lasers are revolutionizing computers.

Lasers also have many uses in business and industry and in everyday life. In factories, lasers are used to cut cloth and harden metals. In supermarkets, a laser at the checkout counter reads the price codes on packages. Lasers are used in our homes in music CD players and videodisc players, which offer much better audio and video reproduction than we get from audiotapes or VCRs.

Lasers have also made a big difference in the way telephones work. Instead of changing sound waves to electricity that travels through copper wire, the most modern telephone technology works by changing sound waves into pulses of laser light that travel through hair-thin glass fibers. One such fiber can carry more than a million conversations at the same time! An added benefit is that this technology lessens the need for copper, a scarce and valuable natural resource.

These are just a few of the thousands of uses for lasers. The laser is truly becoming the light of the twenty-first century.

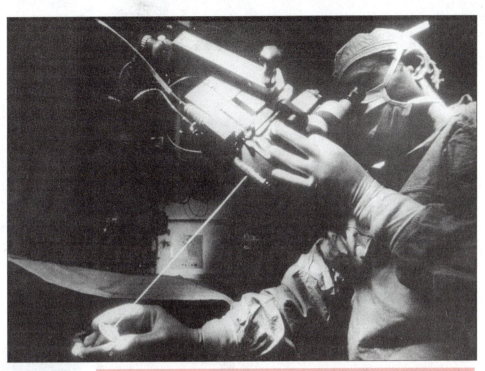

Figure it out

1. **Read the first and last paragraphs of the article. Then say what you think the other paragraphs will be about.**

2. **Read the second and third paragraphs. Then explain in your own words what a laser beam is.**

3. **As you read, pay attention to the different ways lasers are used. When you have finished, give at least three uses of lasers. Then look back at the article and explain in more detail what the laser can do in each case.**

4. **Match.**

1. scarce   a. send
2. application   b. cut
3. device   c. use
4. transmit   d. instrument
5. incision   e. rare

5. **The suffix *-ous* means "possessing or having" and changes a noun into an adjective, as in *cancerous*—"possessing or having cancer." Complete the paragraph, filling in each blank with an appropriate word from the list.**

cancerous   humorous   mysterious
dangerous   marvelous   numerous

About thirty years ago, a laser was a new and _____ device. Now it is clear that laser light has _____ applications. For example, it can remove a _____ growth and prevent its _____ spread to other parts of the body. This _____ device may truly become the light of the twenty-first century.

32. It's not ready yet.

1. Have you ever purchased something expensive, such as a CD player or a television, that didn't work properly? What did you do about it? Tell another student about your experience.

 Jeff Roberts wants to know if his CD player has been repaired yet.

Listen to the conversation.

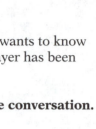

Receptionist	Good morning, Videotronix.
Jeff	Repair Department, please.
Receptionist	Just a moment, please . . . (Rrring, rrring)
Accountant	Televisions. May I help you?
Jeff	Televisions? I asked for the Repair Department.
Accountant	Sorry. Somehow you got switched over here. I'll try to transfer you. . . .
Manager	Repair Department. May I help you?
Jeff	Yes. I'd like to know if my CD player has been repaired yet. It's been more than three weeks. . . .
Manager	What's the ticket number?
Jeff	Uh, let me see. . . . It's J-5412.
Manager	O.K., hold on. . . . Sorry, sir, it's not ready yet.
Jeff	Not yet? It was supposed to have been ready last week. Is there some problem?

Manager	I'm sorry, sir. The parts have been ordered, but they haven't come in yet. The laser mechanism has to be replaced, you know, and it takes a while to get that part. It looks as if it'll be another week.
Jeff	Another week? I'm sorry, but something must be done about this. I want to speak to the manager.
Manager	I *am* the manager, sir.
Jeff	Oh. Well, listen . . . I brought this machine in more than three weeks ago, and I was told it would be ready in two weeks. When I called last week, somebody told me it would be one more week. Now I call and you tell me it's still not ready.
Manager	I'm very sorry, sir. I'll call you just as soon as the repair is finished.
Jeff	Please do. I'll be waiting.

3. What do these sentences mean? Choose *a* or *b*.

1. I'd like to know if my CD player has been repaired yet.
   a. I'd like to know if my CD player is ready.
   b. I'd like to know if there's a problem with my CD player.

2. It was supposed to have been ready last week.
   a. It must have been ready last week.
   b. It should have been ready last week.

3. Something must be done.
   a. Someone must do something.
   b. I told you to do something.

4. It looks as if it'll be another week.
   a. It will probably take a week.
   b. It will take less than a week.

33. It was supposed to have been ready last week.

1
► Listen to the conversation.
► Act out similar conversations with a partner, using the information in the boxes.

Some appliances	
a CD player	a cassette player
a television	a laptop computer

A Repair Department.
B Hello. I'd like to know if my CD player has been repaired yet.
A What's the ticket number?
B Uh, let me see . . . . It's 574-B.
A Just a minute . . . . Sorry, ma'am, it's not ready yet.
B Not yet? It was supposed to have been ready last week. Is there some problem?
A I'm sorry. The parts have been ordered, but they haven't come in yet.

Some ways to complain
It was supposed to have been ready last week.
I was told that it would be ready by now.
I was led to believe that it would be ready in a week.
Is there a reason why it's not ready?
Is there some problem?

Some excuses
The parts have been ordered, but they haven't come in yet.
Two of our repair people are out sick.
We're a little behind schedule at the moment.
Please be patient. We're doing the best we can.

2
► Listen to the conversation.
► Act out similar conversations with a partner. Complain about an urgent problem. Use the information in the box. Your partner will think of a response.

A . . . I need to speak to Mr. Tucker immediately. This is a very urgent matter.
B What's the problem?
A I'm calling for Mrs. Cleary at 45 Hyde Street, Apartment 4D. You know, she's an elderly lady and doesn't feel very well. Her radiator broke two weeks ago and still hasn't been fixed. Something must be done immediately!
B Are you sure the radiator is broken? Maybe it isn't turned on . . . .

Some urgent problems
You live at 45 Hyde Street, and Mrs. Cleary, your neighbor in Apartment 4D, is an elderly lady. Her radiator broke two weeks ago and still hasn't been fixed. Call your landlord, Horace Tucker.
Your roof leaks when it rains, and it hasn't been repaired. When you got home yesterday, water was pouring into your living room. Call your landlord, Joyce Howard.
You are a surgeon and you have to perform an operation this afternoon. There's a problem with the laser surgery device. You called the manufacturer once, and someone was supposed to call you back. Call again and ask to speak to Al Chambers.

Something must be done. = Someone must do something.

THE PASSIVE WITH PRESENT PERFECT VERBS

3 ▶ **Study the frames: The passive with present perfect verbs**

Subject	Present perfect verb	Object
They	**haven't fixed**	my radiator.
We	**'ve notified**	the landlord.
He	**'s sent**	two repair people.
They	**haven't finished**	the repairs.

▶

Subject	Present perfect of *be*	Past participle
My radiator	**hasn't been**	fixed.
The landlord	**has been**	notified.
Two repair people	**have been**	sent.
The repairs	**haven't been**	finished.

same tense

4 ▶ **Helen Fong has brought in her VCR to be repaired. Look at the repair checklist form. Then, using the present perfect, write sentences in the passive that describe which repairs have and haven't been completed.**

The recording heads have (already) been checked. . . .

STATE A PROBLEM

5 ▶ **Helen took her car to a mechanic. Listen to each conversation and decide whether or not it describes a problem. Check (√) the correct column.**

	Problem	Not a problem
1.	_____	_____
2.	_____	_____
3.	_____	_____
4.	_____	_____
5.	_____	_____

6 ▶ Listen to the conversation.

▶ Act out a similar conversation with a partner. Play the role of a customer and describe a problem with something you own. Your partner is a technician and will tell you what he or she thinks is wrong. Use the information in the boxes or your own information.

A Hello, Mr. Snyder. What can I do for you?

B I've brought my car in again. It sounds like a motorboat at full speed.

A *(A few minutes later)* Well, Mr. Snyder, it looks as | if / though | you need a new muffler.

We'll take a closer look and get back to you later today.

B Thanks a lot.

A You bet.

Some problems
Your car sounds like a motorboat at full speed. Your new TV isn't working right. The picture looks like a snowstorm. You're afraid to ride your motorcycle because the engine smells like burning oil. Your cassette player hasn't worked right for the last few days. It sounds like a thunderstorm.

Some evaluations
A customer's car most likely needs a new muffler. A customer's new TV seems to need a new antenna. A customer's motorcycle probably needs a tune-up. A customer's cassette player probably needs to have the heads cleaned.

7 ▶ Study the frame: Sense verbs with *like, as if,* and *as though*

| It | seems
looks
smells
sounds | like | a campfire. | ◀ *like* + noun |
| | | as if
as though | the problem is in the engine. | ◀ *as if* and *as though* + sentence |

8 ▶ Complete the conversations appropriately, using sense verbs with *like, as if,* or *as though* in your answers.

1. **A** Well, the elevator's not working again!
   B Oh, no, not again! *It seems like it breaks down every day* .
   I'm getting tired of this.

2. **A** This stereo sounds terrible.
   B It sure does. _____ .

3. **A** Something smells funny. Is it the oven?
   B I'm not sure, but _____ .

4. **A** My car's been in the shop for repairs five times in the last three months.
   B _____ .

5. **A** What an ugly dog!
   B _____ .

6. **A** This soup tastes awful.
   A Let me try it. Ugh! _____ .

34. Your turn

With a partner, act out conversations for some of these illustrations. Change partners after each conversation, playing Role A in half of your conversations and Role B in the other half. Here are some words you may want to use: *loose, broken, cracked, scratched, stain* (n), *crushed*.

Role A   You purchased one of the items in the illustrations. Later you discovered that something was wrong with it, or something happened to it the first time you used it. Take the item back to the appropriate store and make a complaint. Be careful not to lose your temper, and try to reach an agreement with the store.

Role B   You are the manager of a store, and a customer has come in to complain about an item in the illustrations. Discuss the problem with the customer and reach an agreement.

🔊 Listen in

Two workers at the store where the scratched CD was sold are now discussing audio equipment. Read the statements below. Then listen to the conversation and say *Right* or *Wrong*.

1. The young man wants to get rid of his Univox.
2. The store sells Univox CD players.
3. A Univox CD player is expensive.
4. A Panasound CD player costs at least $400.

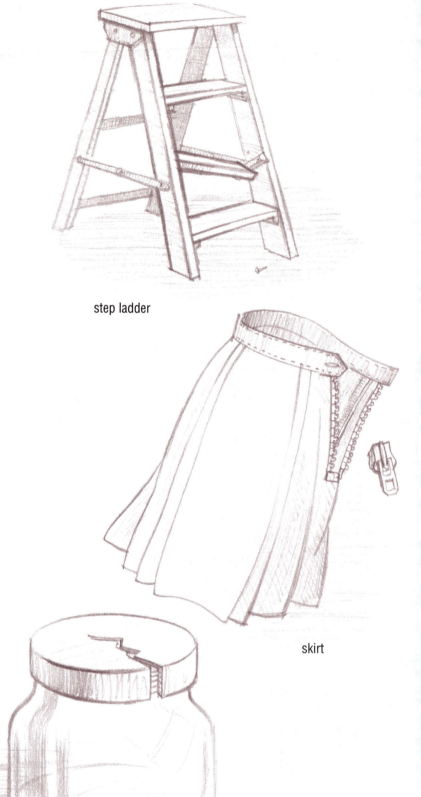

step ladder

skirt

a container

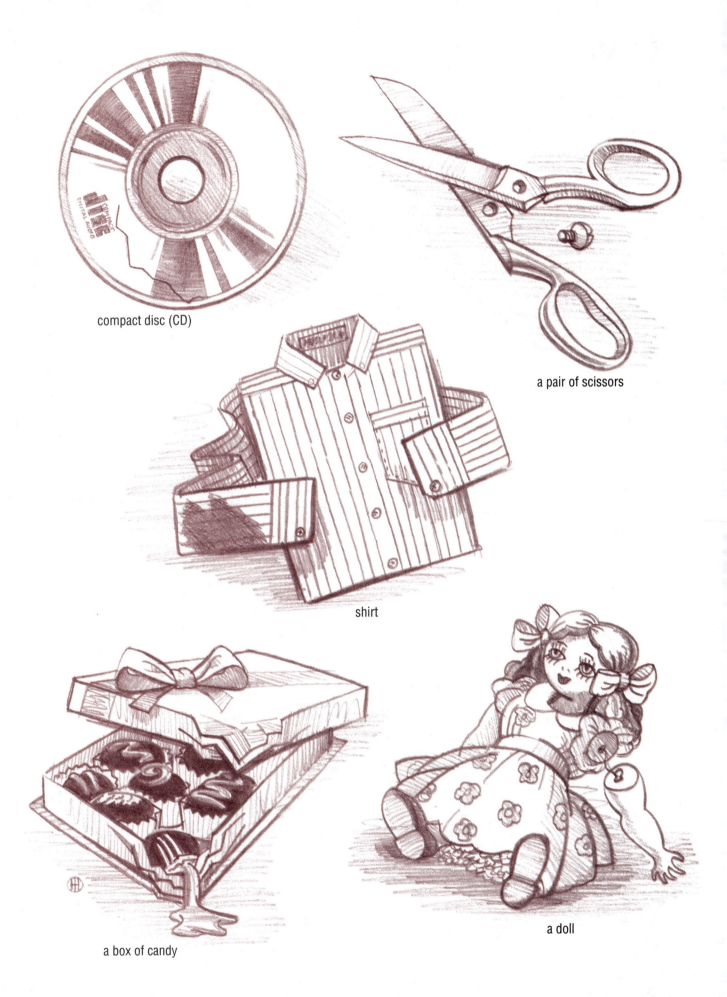

compact disc (CD)

a pair of scissors

shirt

a box of candy

a doll

35. On your own

1. You are the customer relations manager for Univox Audio Systems. Answer the letter of complaint this man wrote to your company.

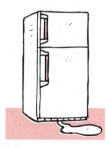

Apartado 519
Panamá, República de Panamá
June 12, 19—

Customer Relations Dept.
Univox Audio Systems, Inc.
7789 Grove Blvd.
Palo Alto, CA 94302

Dear Sir/Madam,

I'm writing to you concerning a Univox CD player (Model CDP 4500) that I purchased several months ago from one of your dealers here in Panama City: Discount Audio.

From your ads, I was led to believe that your audio equipment is the best available on the market. That's hard to believe, considering that I've had nothing but problems with my CD player from the day I bought it.

For one thing, the tracking mechanism doesn't work properly; I can never tell for sure what part of the CD is playing. And now there's a problem with the volume control; sometimes it works and sometimes it doesn't.

I took the player to the service department at Discount Audio. When I picked it up, they said they'd fixed the tracking mechanism as best they could, but it still doesn't work properly.

I'm sick and tired of all the problems I've had with your product. I hope you will understand my concern. I look forward to hearing from you about what you can do to help solve this problem.

Sincerely yours,

Roberto Suárez
Roberto Suárez

2. Write a letter of complaint about something you've had a problem with recently. You may write to an appliance store, a grocery store, a department store, your landlord, an airline, a bus company, or any other appropriate place.

FUNCTIONS/THEMES	LANGUAGE	FORMS
Make comparisons	Some people think scuba diving is exciting. A lot more people get hurt walking down the street each year than scuba diving.	Quantifiers Comparisons with quantifiers
Compare opinions	Auto racing must be really exciting. Oh, I don't know about that. It's pretty dangerous. Maybe so, but it appeals to a lot of people. Some of them keep doing it even after they get injured.	Quantifiers with *of*

Preview the reading.

1. Work with a partner. Discuss the danger involved in each of the scenes below. If you've ever participated in a dangerous sport, tell your partner about it.

2. Before you read the article on page 80, look at the title and the photos on pages 80–81. What do you think the article is about? Discuss your answer with a partner.

DANGER FOR THE FUN OF IT

by Judy Klemesrud

Dennis Joyce is a 30-year-old employee of an electric company in New York City. To put some excitement into his life, he spends many weekends and vacations white-water canoeing. He is one of the growing number of Americans who in recent years have taken up dangerous sports to fill their leisure hours.

Although he has fallen into the river several times, Mr. Joyce has never been hurt himself. Yet he admits he has seen some very serious accidents.

People who participate in risky sports usually have several things in common. Most are men. They don't like others to think of them as thrill seekers, yet they admit the dangers of their sport. And almost all of them look down on sports like tennis and golf.

"There's just nothing happening in sports like tennis and golf," said Steve Kaufman, a 44-year-old Manhattan bill collector who scuba dives in his spare time. According to him, the only people who come close to the experience of scuba divers are astronauts "because they're in a totally alien environment, too." Kaufman describes his sport as "a total isolation from anything that can interfere with your own personal sense of self."

Mr. Kaufman said his most dangerous moment as a diver came when he found himself looking at about 800 to 900 sharks. Fortunately, he got out of there really fast.

George Weigel, a 31-year-old carpenter from Pawling, New York, enjoys hang gliding. Although many risk-takers see hang gliding as the most dangerous sport of all, Weigel feels hang gliders should not be regarded as thrill seekers. Yet he said that hang gliding "scares the living daylights out of me" and that "everything else seems boring compared to it."

Why do people willingly seek out danger? According to Dr. George Serban, associate professor of clinical psychiatry at New York University, most men do it to prove their masculinity.

"The nature of the male animal is to undertake dangerous tasks and to confront them and to succeed," Dr. Serban said. When life becomes boring and routine, Serban says, and men do not have a chance for adventure or a chance to prove their masculinity, the only other possibility for them is to undertake dangerous activities.

Eric D. Rosenfeld, a 43-year-old Manhattan lawyer who has been climbing mountains for 20 years, spoke of the habit-forming nature of his sport. "It's quite addictive," he says. "You get addicted to the risk factor."

In recent years, Mr. Rosenfeld has been climbing mountains in the Arctic. He contrasts the mountains in the Arctic with some in Europe. In Europe, he said, there are lines of people waiting to go up sections of mountains, guides walking around, and garbage all over the place. "In the Arctic no one's around. There's no such thing as a guide because no one's ever been there."

Although several of his friends have died while mountain climbing, Rosenfeld said, "I have an intellectual appreciation that it's risky. But I sit in my law office and tell myself that after 20 years of climbing I'm still here."

The novelty of the sport is what attracted Susan Tripp, a 35-year-old Manhattan lawyer, to skin-diving. She likes it because it "is not something many people do." That is also one of the main reasons John Wolcott, a 49-year-old printer from Edison, New Jersey, likes to go hot air ballooning. "It makes me a hero," he said. At parties, he said, he simply introduces ballooning into the conversation, and he becomes the center of attention for at least an hour.

Figure it out

1. Answer these questions.

1. What is the main idea of the article?
2. What are the names of the people in the article who participate in dangerous sports, and what sports do they participate in?
3. What reasons do they give for participating in these sports?
4. Why do you think they participate in such dangerous sports?

2. As you read, pay attention to the characteristics that people who like dangerous sports have in common. When you have finished, say *Right* or *Wrong* for each statement below and correct the wrong statements.

People who participate in dangerous sports . . .
1. often don't think that they're dangerous.
2. almost always think sports like tennis and golf are boring.
3. usually are men.
4. want to feel more masculine.
5. generally don't like to talk about their sport.
6. sometimes find the sport habit-forming.

3. The people interviewed in this article make some interesting comments. Below are some of them. Do you agree or disagree with each of them? Explain why.

1. "There's just nothing happening in sports like tennis and golf."
2. "The nature of the male animal is to undertake dangerous tasks and to confront them and to succeed."
3. "[Participating in a dangerous sport] makes me a hero."

4. There are many expressions in English that contain the verb *look*. Complete the paragraph with appropriate expressions from the list.

look down on	= have a bad opinion of
look up to	= admire
look for	= try to find
look at	= see
look up	= get in touch with someone or try to find out a fact
look over	= examine quickly

    Carmen Perez is the center of attention at parties. People _____ her because she goes hot-air ballooning. Carmen used to play tennis, but she started to _____ a new sport because "tennis was too boring." One day an old friend _____ Carmen, and suggested she try ballooning. Carmen loves her new sport. "I guess now I even _____ sports like tennis," she admits.

37. I've taken up scuba diving.

1. Compare some of the popular sports where you live. Which ones can be dangerous? How? Which do you like the best? Why?

Dan is talking to his friends Linda and Toni about his new hobby, scuba diving.

Listen to the conversation.

2

Linda Hey, Dan, how's it going? We hear you've got a new hobby.

Dan Yeah, I've taken up scuba diving.

Linda That must be a lot of fun. Maybe we should try it, Toni.

Toni Huh? You think I'm nuts? It's supposed to be really dangerous, isn't it?

Dan Well, maybe a little, but it sure is a change from working here in the store.

Linda Are you saying this job is boring?

Dan Compared to scuba diving, it is. After all, you can't exactly say there's much excitement around here.

Toni Except when the manager catches us talking. . . . You know, I was just reading about scuba diving in some magazine. Two or three percent of divers get attacked by sharks.

Dan Oh, come on. You can't believe half of what you read in magazines. Do you realize that scuba diving is less risky than boating?

Linda Yeah. Listen, many people dive, and most of them never have any trouble.

Toni Maybe not, but I still think it's dangerous.

Dan And did you know that fewer people get scuba hurt diving than walking down the street?

Toni Sure. Tell me another one.

Linda No, he's right. And do you know where there are even more risks than in the water or on the street?

Toni No, where?

Linda Right here in the supermarket. Every day they find out that something else we buy here and eat is bad for us!

Toni Ha ha, very funny. . . . Hey, I'd better get back to work before the boss starts complaining. Catch you two later.

Linda O.K. Let's talk more about it when we have our break.

3. Complete the sentences, using *more*, *many*, or *much*.

1. _____ people enjoy scuba diving.
2. There isn't _____ danger in scuba diving.
3. _____ people get hurt walking down the street than scuba diving.
4. There are _____ risks in the food we eat than walking down the street.
5. _____ sports are safe if you're careful.

38. Some people think scuba diving is exciting.

MAKE COMPARISONS • QUANTIFIERS

1 ▶ **Listen to the two possible conversations.**
   ▶ **Act out similar conversations with a partner, using the information in the boxes.**

You'd like to . . .
take up scuba diving. move to a big city. look for a job as a _____ .

A I'm thinking of taking up scuba diving. It would be exciting.
B Isn't it kind of dangerous, though? You could get attacked by a shark.
A Listen, a lot more people get hurt walking down the street each year than scuba diving.

B Well, I guess you have a point.   **B** | Maybe so, but
Even so, | I still wouldn't recommend it.

Some reservations
Scuba diving could be dangerous. You could get attacked by a shark. The city is a poor place to raise children. There's a lot of crime there. _____ is a bad field to look for work in these days. There are very few opportunities/very few jobs that pay well.

Some comparisons
A lot more people get hurt walking down the street each year than scuba diving. There's less danger after dark on a busy city street than on a deserted country road. There are fewer qualified _____ now than ever before.

You could get attacked by a shark. = A shark could attack you.

2 ▶ **Study the frames: Quantifiers**

Quantifiers with count and mass nouns		
A lot of **Most** **Many** **Some** **Not many** **A few** **Few**	people	think scuba diving is exciting.

▲
count noun

A *few* and *a little* vs. *few* and *little*
Few and *little* emphasize the smallness of the quantity more than *a few* and *a little*. Compare: There *a little* excitement in baseball. (It's not that boring.) There's *little* excitement in baseball. (It's pretty boring.) *A few* and *a little* are modified by *only*, whereas *few* and *little* are modified by *very*: *Only* a few people went to the game. *Very few* people enjoyed themselves.

A lot of **Most** **Some** **Not much** **A little** **Little**	food	is bad for you.

▲
mass noun

Many may be used in affirmative statements. However, *much* is generally used only in negative statements.

There's little excitement in baseball. Only a few people went to the game.

3 ▶ **Listen to the conversation.**
▶ **Act out similar conversations with a partner. Compare two sports, using the information in the boxes and your own information.**

A Do you ever play tennis?
B Hardly ever. I've only played a few times. I'd rather go jogging.
A There isn't much excitement in jogging.
B But on the other hand, you get just as much exercise and you can do it by yourself. What's more, you don't have to buy expensive equipment.
A What about those expensive warm-up suits?
B All you really need are running shoes. . . .

Some sports	Some considerations
tennis/jogging	action
scuba diving/	exercise
hang gliding	equipment
boxing/wrestling	special clothing
walking/jogging	expense
baseball/soccer	time
basketball/tennis	injuries
	danger

4 ▶ **Study the frames: Comparisons with quantifiers**

Boxers have	**more**			wrestlers.
Wrestlers have	**fewer**	injuries	**than**	boxers.

▲ count noun

Soccer has	**more**			baseball.
Baseball has	**less**	action	**than**	soccer.

▲ mass noun

Joggers have just	**as many**			tennis players.
Scuba divers have just	**as few**	injuries	**as**	swimmers.

▲ count noun

Swimmers get just	**as much**			joggers.
My sister gets just	**as little**	exercise	**as**	my parents.

▲ mass noun

5 ▶ **Complete the article with the appropriate quantifiers or comparisons with quantifiers. Some items have more than one answer.**

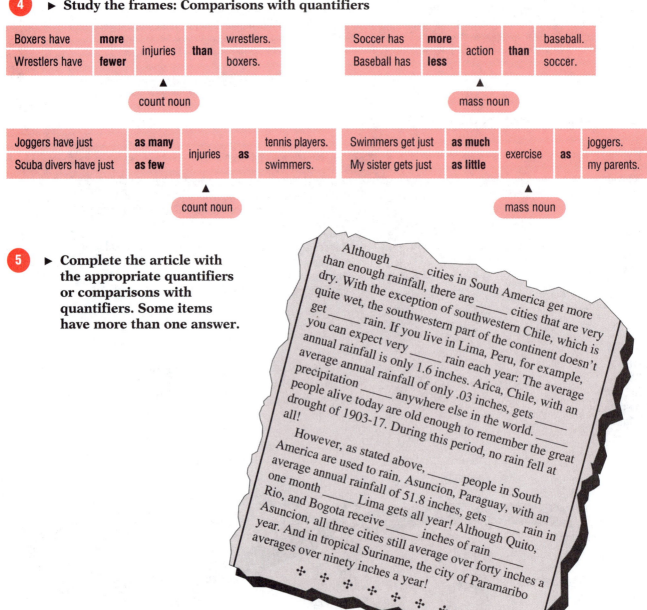

Although _____ cities in South America get more than enough rainfall, there are _____ cities that are very dry. With the exception of southwestern Chile, which is quite wet, the southwestern part of the continent doesn't get _____ rain. If you live in Lima, Peru, for example, you can expect very _____ rain each year: The average annual rainfall is only 1.6 inches. Arica, Chile, with an average annual rainfall of only .03 inches, gets _____ precipitation _____ anywhere else in the world. _____ people alive today are old enough to remember the great drought of 1903–17. During this period, no rain fell at all!

However, as stated above, _____ people in South America are used to rain. Asuncion, Paraguay, with an average annual rainfall of 51.8 inches, gets _____ one month _____ Lima gets all year! Although Quito, Rio, and Bogota receive _____ rain in Asuncion, all three cities still average over forty inches a year. And in tropical Suriname, the city of Paramaribo averages over ninety inches a year!

❖ ❖ ❖ ❖ ❖ ❖ ❖

6 ▶ **Listen to the conversations. Does the second speaker agree or disagree with the first speaker? Check (√) the appropriate column.**

Agree   Disagree

1. _____   _____
2. _____   _____
3. _____   _____
4. _____   _____
5. _____   _____

7 ▶ **Listen to the conversation.**
    ▶ **Act out similar conversations with a partner, using the information in the boxes or your own information. Take turns expressing opinions and agreeing or disagreeing.**

A Auto racing must be really exciting.
B Oh, I don't know about that. It's pretty dangerous.
A Maybe so, but it appeals to a lot of people. Some of them keep doing it even after they get injured.

> **Some opinions**
>
> Auto racing must be really exciting. Some people keep doing it even after they get injured.
> Many talented artists don't get the respect they deserve. Only a few of them make a good salary.
> Most courses are too easy. Many of them are really interesting, but they're not challenging enough.
> A lot of people get married too young. Many of them are very unhappy afterwards.

> In informal conversation, you may form the passive with *get* rather than *be*.
>   They *get* injured = They *are* injured.

> **Some topics**
>
> sports   school
> jobs   marriage
> your values (what's important to you)

8 ▶ **Study the frames: Quantifiers with *of***

count noun		
A lot of	people	I know go scuba diving.
All Many Most Some A few None	of them	have been injured.

mass noun		
A lot of	money	is spent on sports.
All Most Some Much A little None	of it	is wasted.

Two	people	I know go scuba diving.
Both	of them	have been injured.
One Neither		has been injured.

9. ▶ **What foods do people like in your country? Write a paragraph using quantifiers and quantifiers with *of*.**

Start like this:

Most people in ____ like ____ .
Many of them like ____ more than ____ . . . .

39. Your turn

You are on a committee that is in charge of selecting sports for school athletic programs. Work in groups to compare the sports in the photos and then decide if the schools should adopt any of them. Make sure to take into account each of the considerations in the box from exercise 3 on p. 80.

A *Basketball is certainly less dangerous than football, right?*
B *Yes, and I think it's less expensive, too.*

basketball

🔊 Listen in

Parents Against Dangerous Sports (PADS) has paid a local radio station to air its editorial. Read the paragraph below. Then listen to the editorial and fill in each blank with the correct sport.

PADS believes that _____ has no place in school athletic programs. Its members want to replace _____ with _____ . The group argues that _____ isn't as dangerous as _____ . In fact, _____ and not _____ is played in most countries.

track and field

soccer

tennis

swimming

motorcycle racing

football

40. On your own

1. Compare yourself to Tetsuo or to Annette.

- Tetsuo eats twice a day.
- He drinks at least three glasses of water a day.
- It takes him fifty minutes to get to work.
- It takes only ten minutes for him to get to school.
- He gets twenty minutes of exercise a week.
- He spends more time away from home than at home.
- He has one brother and two sisters.

I eat more often than Tetsuo.
I drink less water than he does. It . . .

- Annette eats four light meals a day.
- She drinks at least five glasses of water a day.
- It takes her ten minutes to get to work.
- It takes thirty minutes for her to get to school.
- She gets three hours of exercise a week.
- She spends more time at home than away from home.
- She has two brothers and three sisters.

I eat fewer meals than Annette.
I drink less water than she does. It . . .

2. What's your opinion about sports in schools? Do you think the schools where you live put too much or too little emphasis on sports? Write a letter to the person in charge of sports in your schools, comparing the current sports program with the one you feel should replace it.

FUNCTIONS/THEMES	LANGUAGE	FORMS
Make a complaint	The noise has been driving me crazy. I just wish something could be done about it.	The passive with modal auxiliaries in present or future time
Offer to do something	I'll get the restaurant to send up a sandwich for you. I'll get a sandwich sent up to you.	The causative *get* in active and passive sentences
Give advice	Maybe you're just hungry. I've read that eating something high in protein can help.	

Preview the reading.

1. Have you ever been in a situation like those in the illustration below? Tell your partner about your favorite remedy for a headache or other remedies you know about.

2. Before you read the article on pages 90–91, look at the title and the illustrations. Then work with a partner to discuss the significance of the illustrations and to guess what the article is about.

41. Headache Away

by Marian Wolbers

When you have a headache, do you rush to your medicine cabinet or to the drugstore for a pain reliever? If so, you're not alone. People in the United States spend over $2 billion a year on nonprescription pain relievers. Although effective, these pain relievers are not without problems. First of all, which should you choose? There are over 100 brands, and most come in various forms (for example, tablets or capsules) and various strengths (such as regular and extra strength). Choosing a pain reliever can be enough to make anyone's headache worse! Second, the 100-plus brands fall into three types of pain relievers—aspirin, acetaminophen, and ibuprofen—and each of these can have serious side effects. Aspirin and ibuprofen can cause stomach irritation and gastrointestinal bleeding; acetaminophen can cause liver damage in some people.

So, next time you have a headache, instead of rushing to the drugstore, you might want to try one of these natural headache remedies:

1. Eat something soon. Preferably, eat something high in protein, a substance necessary for growth. The "hungry headache," caused by a drop in the blood-sugar supply, can be a real problem for people not eating enough at mealtimes. Why protein? Because it rebuilds your blood-sugar supply little by little. Sugary foods cause the blood sugar to go up rapidly and then drop again just as fast.

2. Wash it away. At the first sign of headache pain, get in the shower, advises Dr. Augustus S. Rose of the UCLA (University of California at Los Angeles) School of Medicine. First take a hot shower even if the pain gets worse. This will make the blood vessels open wide. Follow it immediately with a cold shower. Stay in until you shiver. Repeat this procedure if necessary. This process works well for a migraine headaches. In a migraine headache, the blood vessels of the head first contract (get smaller), then dilate (open up) and press against the nerves. This pressure causes pain. Cold water makes the blood vessels contract, which eases this pressure on the nerves.

3. Freeze it out. If you are miles away from the shower, Dr. Rose suggests putting crushed ice in your mouth. Again, this is useful for a migraine headache. However, this remedy is inappropriate for elderly or sick people.

4. Think it away. Sit down or lie down and close your eyes. Imagine that it is summer and you are on the beach. An ocean breeze cools your face and your hands and arms grow warmer and warmer in the hot sun. Your hands are really soaking up the sun. They become hot to the touch. Minutes pass, and when you open your eyes, you are left with very warm hands . . . and no headache. Thinking warmth into your hands sends blood toward them and away from the head.

5. Massage it out. Get to your head through your feet. Massaging the lower part of your big toe and the area under all your toes will lessen tension in the neck. This tension can often cause a headache.

6. Breathe it away. According to Dr. Selwyn Dexter, breathing into an ordinary paper bag can get rid of migraine headaches caused by hyperventilation. (Hyperventilation is a condition in which breathing is usually fast or deep.) Simply breathe into a paper bag and rebreathe the same air, which is mostly carbon dioxide. This process may take as long as 15 minutes, Dr. Dexter says, but it has worked for several of his patients.

7. Press it away. Some headaches can be cured by a sensitive finger-pressure massage. The massage should be given on sensitive "trigger" points. There are three pairs of points: one at each temple, one under each shoulder blade, and a pair at the back of the neck. Press each point for 15 to 30 seconds at a time. Remember to press both points in a pair at the same time, not just one side. Doing this will help the body's natural painkillers start working. If you are alone, press the thumb of one hand against the tender spot in the "V" formed by the thumb and forefinger of the other hand.

8. Brush it away. Find a hairbrush with fairly stiff natural bristles, says biophysicist Harry C. Ehrmantraut. Then use the following procedure, first on one side of your head and then on the other: Starting a little above your temple, just above your eyebrow, brush you hair in small circles. Move the brush first up and then back before moving it down and forward to complete you circle. This way the upper part of the circle goes toward the back of the head. Then brush your hair in circles around your ear, and finally brush down to the base of your skull.

After you repeat this procedure on the other side of your head, brush the hair in the center of your scalp, first on the right and then on the left. Make small circles as you start at the top of your head and move down toward the base of your skull. Brushing stimulates the skin and the tissues underneath so blood can flow more easily and more oxygen can reach the brain. **Always see a doctor for continuous or recurring head pain.**

Figure it out

1. Read the questions. Then read the article and answer them.

1. What are three types of nonprescription pain relievers available in many drugstores?
2. What does brushing the hair do to the skin to help relieve a headache?
3. How could eating a steak help get rid of a headache?
4. How can you "press a headache away"?
5. Do you ever hyperventilate? What can hyperventilation cause?

2. As you read, try to remember the important facts about each remedy. When you have finished, choose *a* or *b* for each statement below. Then describe in your own words the two remedies that you feel are the most practical and effective.

1. Eat something soon.
   a. Eat something high in protein.
   b. Eat something with sugar in it.

2. Wash it away.
   a. Take a cold shower.
   b. Take a hot shower and then a cold one right after it.

3. Freeze it out.
   a. Hold ice against your forehead.
   b. Put crushed ice in your mouth and throat.

4. Think it away.
   a. Imagine that your hands are getting very warm.
   b. Imagine that your head is getting very warm.

5. Massage it out.
   a. Massage the area under your toes.
   b. Massage your neck.

6. Breathe it away.
   a. Go outside and breathe fresh air.
   b. Breathe into a paper bag.

7. Press it away.
   a. Have someone apply pressure to sensitive spots on both sides of your head.
   b. Have someone apply pressure to the side of your head that hurts the most.

8. Brush it away.
   a. Brush the back of your head near your neck.
   b. Brush both sides of your head, moving from the front to the back.

3. The words *away* and *out* are often used to form two-word verbs meaning "to get rid of something," as in *wash away* (a headache) or *freeze out* (a headache). Complete the paragraph, using a direct object and an appropriate two-word verb from the article. Remember that when the direct object is a pronoun it is placed between the two words.

There are many natural remedies for a headache. You can _____ by taking a shower, but if you're not near a shower, you can _____ with ice. People who are elderly or sick should not try to _____ , however. You can also _____ with a fairly stiff hairbrush or have a friend _____ for you with his or her fingers. If you imagine that you are lying in the hot sun, you can even _____ .

42. My head is killing me!

1. What are some situations that give you a headache? Discuss different remedies with your partner.

Dennis and Stan work for a mail-order company. It's just before the holidays, and they're very busy.

Listen to the conversation.

2

Dennis I don't see any more bags. All the orders must be sorted, finally. I'm dead!

Stan No, I'm afraid there are two more bags left.

Dennis Two more! My feet are ready to drop off, and I'm stressed out.

Stan Well, after the holidays things will slow down.

Dennis I hope I last that long. . . . Something should be done about that noise outside. It's really impossible to work in here.

Stan It *is* annoying. Still, it's a good thing they're fixing the sidewalk.

Dennis They'd better fill that hole. Someone could get killed.

Stan I hope they get it all done by tomorrow.

Dennis If they don't, I'm going to go nuts.

Stan Huh? Are you all right, Dennis?

Dennis Yes, I mean, no. My head is killing me, and that noise is driving me crazy!

Stan Maybe you'd better work over there in the corner.

Dennis No, the radio is louder than the drill.

Stan Look, I'll get them to turn it down.

Dennis No, don't go to any trouble! I'll just take some aspirin.

Stan And try to relax a bit, O.K.?

Dennis I know. I really have to calm down. I'm probably giving *you* a headache.

Stan Hey, we all have our bad days.

3. Find another way to say it.

1. Someone should do something about that noise outside.
2. I'll have them turn it down.
3. I have a bad headache, and I can't stand that noise.
4. It could kill someone.
5. I hope they finish it all by tomorrow.

43. I just wish something could be done about it.

1 ▸ Listen to the conversation.
  ▸ Act out a similar conversation with a partner, using the information in the boxes or your own information.

A They're doing construction right outside my bedroom window, and the noise has been driving me crazy.
B I know how you feel. I had that problem at work once.
A I just wish something could be done about it, though. It wakes me up at seven every Saturday.
B Well, what if you slept with earplugs?
A Now that's a thought.

Some sources of noise	Some comments on a proposal
construction airplanes traffic dogs neighbors coworkers	Now that's a thought. It's worth a try. I guess it doesn't hurt to try.
	It's not worth the effort. It's more trouble than it's worth. It's too much of a headache.

2 ▸ Listen to the discussion at a neighborhood meeting.
  Check (√) the problems that the people expect to be fixed by next month.

3 ▸ Study the frames: The passive with modal auxiliaries in present and future time

Active			
Someone	must	fix	the sidewalk.
Someone	should	fix	the sidewalk.
The repairs	could would	prevent	an accident.
That big hole	may might	injure	someone.
That big hole	must	annoy	people.
Someone	can	fix	the sidewalk.
You	may can	file	a complain.
Someone	will	repair	the sidewalk.

an obligation	
a recommendation	
a result	
a possibility	
a logical conclusion	
ability	
permission	
future time	

◂ ▸

Passive			
The sidewalk	**must**		fixed.
The sidewalk	**should**		fixed.
An accident	**could would**		prevented.
Someone	**may might**	**be**	injured.
People	**must**		annoyed.
The sidewalk	**can**		fixed.
A complaint	**may can**		filed.
The sidewalk	**will**		repaired.

base form ▲

past participle ▲

Use *could* for a possible result and *would* for a more definite result. Compare:
If they fixed the hole in the sidewalk . . .
  an accident *could* be prevented. (It's possible.)
  an accident *would* be prevented. (I'm sure of it.)

Unit 9 **93**

4
▶ **Listen to the conversation.**
▶ **Act out a similar conversation with a partner, using the information in the boxes or your own information.**

A Did you notice the hole in the sidewalk outside this building?
B Yes. Someone could fall and break a leg.
A It really should be filled.

Some dangers
a hole in the sidewalk
a pothole on a highway
broken glass on the floor of a store
water on the floor of a restaurant

You *fill* a hole, *fix* a pothole, *sweep up* glass, and *mop up* water.

5
▶ **Write a letter of complaint to the traffic department, using at least three sentences with modal auxiliaries. Use the information from the list.**

Start like this:

Dear Sir/Madam:

I am writing to express my concern about a dangerous intersection at Warren Street and Porter Avenue. . . .

Information to include:
Problems at Warren St. and Porter Ave.
• five accidents in three months—no traffic light or stop sign
• parked cars on both sides of the street—hard to see pedestrians
• school crossing (Porter Elementary School on Porter Ave.)—no crossing guard
Solutions
• install traffic light or stop signs
• prohibit parking on these streets
• assign a crossing guard to the intersection before and after school

6
▶ **Listen to the conversation.**
▶ **Act out a similar conversation with a partner, using the information in the box or your own information.**

A I'm starving, but I don't have time to go out for lunch.

B I'll get | the restaurant to send up a sandwich / a sandwich sent up | for you.

A Oh, you don't have to do that.
B It's really no trouble at all.

Some situations
It's already two o'clock in the afternoon and you have too much work to do to go out for lunch.
You're in the hospital and you just noticed that your pitcher of water is empty.
You want to park your car, but a delivery truck is blocking your driveway.
It's very hot in the restaurant where you're having dinner, but the air conditioner isn't turned on.

7 ▶ **Study the frames: The causative *get***

Active				
They're trying to	**get**	me you him her us them	to fix	the radiator.
			to stop	the noise.

▲ infinitive

Passive			
They're trying to	**get**	the radiator	fixed.
		the noise	stopped.

▲ past participle

Compare:
They're trying to *have* him *fix* the radiator.
They're trying to *get* him *to fix* the radiator.

8 ▶ **Alberto Lopez, who manages a drugstore, is talking to Sheila Evans, the assistant manager. Complete Sheila's part of the conversation, using the causative *get* or the causative *have* in either active or passive sentences.**

Alberto We're low on aspirin.
 Sheila Yes, I know. I'll talk to the supplier and *get him to send an order right away./ have an order sent right away.*
Alberto Good, because the order may take up to a week to come in.
 Sheila Speaking of orders, they sent an order of shampoo to our other store by mistake. Do you want me to _____ ?
Alberto Sure. Why should we have to pick it up?
By the way, someone should unpack those two crates of deodorant in the back.
 Sheila O.K. I'll _____ .
Alberto Jim won't be in today. Ask Harry.
Hey, what's that puddle back there?
 Sheila Oh, someone broke a bottle of cough medicine. I'll _____ .
Alberto One last thing. Bonnie forgot to fill out her timecard last week. Please talk to her about it.
 Sheila Don't worry. I'll _____ .

 9 ▶ **Listen to the conversation.**
 ▶ **Act out a similar conversation with a partner, using the information in the boxes and in the article on pages 86–87.**

A My head is killing me!
B Maybe you're just hungry. What time did you eat lunch?
A I didn't. I was too busy to take a break.
B Hunger is a common cause of headaches. I've read that eating something high in protein can help.

Some causes of headaches	Some situations
hunger	You had a busy day at work or school and didn't eat lunch.
eyestrain	You've been studying in the library all day.
noise	You and a friend are at a rock concert.
nervousness	You have the lead role in a play and are about to go on stage.
sun	You've been repairing telephone lines outdoors all day in the hot sun.

44. Your turn

You have gotten together with a group of neighbors to complain about the "headaches" in these pictures. Work in groups to find solutions to each one.

Rate the amount of stress each of the following situations causes you. (0 = no stress; 1 = slight stress; 2 = medium stress; 3 = a lot of stress) Then discuss your answers with a partner. Give each other advice about how to reduce stress in each situation.

___ Your best friend moves away to a different city, far from where you live.
___ You lose your job.
___ You fail an exam at school.
___ A close relative dies suddenly.
___ You oversleep and miss an important meeting.
___ You get caught in a traffic jam and know you'll be late for class.
___ You have to move to another country to work for a branch of your company. You'd rather stay where you are.

🔊 Listen in

Read the question below. Then listen to the interview and choose *a*, *b*, *c*, or *d*.

How did Mr. Hatfield solve the problem of his neighbor's yard?

a. He got his neighbor to clean up the yard.
b. He got the yard cleaned up himself.
c. He called the police.
d. He wasn't able to solve the problem.

Do you agree with the conclusion Mr. Hatfield reached? Discuss this question in groups.

45. On your own

1. **Read the letter Mark wrote to his friend Sara. Then answer it, giving advice.**

2. **Write a letter of complaint to your community newspaper. Complain about a real problem in your neighborhood. Try to suggest more than one solution for it.**

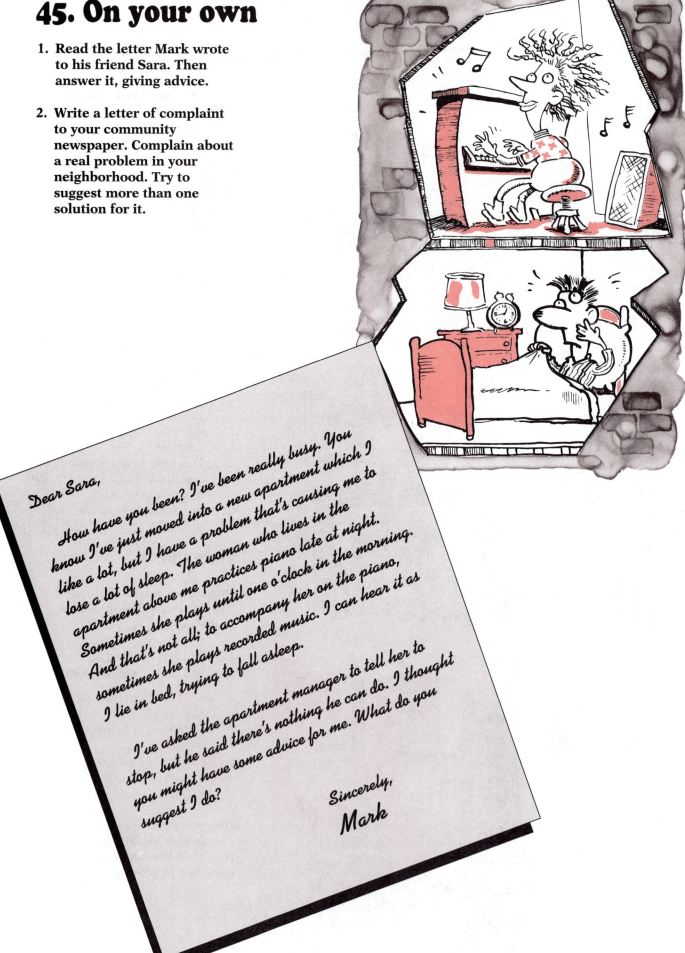

Dear Sara,

How have you been? I've been really busy. You know I've just moved into a new apartment which I like a lot, but I have a problem that's causing me to lose a lot of sleep. The woman who lives in the apartment above me practices piano late at night. Sometimes she plays until one o'clock in the morning. And that's not all; to accompany her on the piano, sometimes she plays recorded music. I can hear it as I lie in bed, trying to fall asleep.

I've asked the apartment manager to tell her to stop, but he said there's nothing he can do. I thought you might have some advice for me. What do you suggest I do?

Sincerely,
Mark

PREVIEW

FUNCTIONS/THEMES	LANGUAGE	FORMS
Imagine the future Talk about the future	I wonder what I'll be doing in five years. In twenty years, I'll buy a house by the seashore.	The future with *will* vs. the future continuous with *will*
Discuss possibilities Express regret	Would you ever play the lottery? If I had extra money, I would. If I'd gone to journalism school, I could have been a TV reporter.	Contrary-to-fact conditional sentences

Preview the reading.

1. What kind of tickets are shown in the photo? Can you buy similar tickets in your country? Have you ever bought any? Have you ever won any money that way?

2. Before you read the article on pages 100–101, look at the title and the photos on page 100. Discuss with a partner what you think the article is about.
3. A lottery is a game in which people buy a ticket with a number or numbers on it in hopes of winning a lot of money. What would you do if you won a million dollars in a lottery?

WINNING THE LOTTERY

... Is It a Dream Come True?

Gloria Mitchem

Most people have found themselves daydreaming about winning a million dollars—as a solution to their money problems or as a path to happiness and a life of luxury. As more and more states set up lottery games, more and more people rush to buy a ticket and a dream. The states view lotteries as a way to make money, since only about half of what they take in is given back as prize money. The prize is usually broken down into as many as twenty smaller, yearly payments instead of one huge payment.

Because there are so many types of lottery games, and they all have winners, it can seem like a very easy thing to win—especially in those rare cases where someone has won more than one game. But in reality, the odds of winning the lottery are very small. In fact, you are more likely to be struck by lightning than to become an instant millionaire.

Shellah Ryan

But what about those lucky few who do win? Have they achieved the American dream—are they on easy street? It's fun to picture these winners quitting their jobs, going on a wild shopping spree, and spending a lifetime traveling around the world. But according to a survey, most people who win keep their jobs, stay in their neighborhoods and keep the same friends, and they're careful about how they spend their money.

When Christene Cooper won $19 million in the California lottery, she was a 20-year-old student working two jobs. According to Christene, "Winning was pretty unbelievable; it changes so much in your life." Because they were able to afford to live on their own, she and her high school sweetheart got married. They went to Disney World on their honeymoon, and they bought a BMW convertible, a truck, and a yacht. She bought houses for relatives and set up a trust fund for her sister.

Sheelah Ryan won $55.5 million in the Florida lottery. A retired real estate agent, she continues to live a basically modest lifestyle despite the $2.8 million she receives every year. She replaced her trailer home with a beautiful house and bought a luxury car, but she also started a foundation in honor of her parents. The Ryan Foundation sets up programs to assist single mothers and senior citizens who need financial help. In addition, she gives out small scholarships to needy students. According to Sheelah, "We have a responsibility to help those who need help. I'm grateful that I can."

For Gloria Mitchem, winning the Florida lottery prize of $37.4 million was more of a problem than a blessing. She was living in a small town and working in a nursing home when she found out she was a winner. By the next day, crowds of people and reporters were outside her home. She needed a police escort to take her to claim the prize. Then, after a press conference when relatives mentioned that they'd like to buy a fancy car, automobile salesmen started hounding her along with the press. Gloria decided she had had enough and needed to be left alone. She quit her job, took her child out of day care, and left town.

She refuses to speak to reporters, and only her family and a few close friends know where she now lives.

Even the lottery agencies recognize that winning can open the door to worry as well as happiness. They advise winners to at least get new phone numbers if they can't move. They also recommend getting a good lawyer and financial advisor. To win the lottery you only need luck, but to manage the changes in your life that come with the jackpot, you need lots of planning and good advice.

Figure it out

1. Read the first and last paragraphs of the article. What do you suppose the main idea of the article is?

2. Read the entire article and answer these questions.

1. Why do states set up lottery games?
2. How likely is it that you will win the lottery?
3. All three lottery winners bought a certain item after they won. What is the item?
4. Which lottery winner—Christene Cooper, Sheelah Ryan, or Gloria Mitchem—do you think is happiest today? Why?

3. Find the highlighted words and say what they refer to. The words are listed below in the order in which they appear.

1. It	5. They
2. they	6. I
3. you	7. her
4. their	8. you

4. Decide who would make each comment below. Say *Christene Cooper, Sheelah Ryan,* or *Gloria Mitchem.*

1. I'm thankful, not only for the money I received, but for the opportunity to help people in need.
2. My boyfriend and I always wanted to take a trip on one of those cruise ships. Now we don't have to because we have our own big boat.
3. I had to ask myself over and over "Is this really true? Did I really win the lottery?"
4. The last thing I need is for some newspaper reporter to find out where I live.
5. I want my mother and father to be remembered through my good deeds.
6. Please keep my address and phone number to yourself.

5. The suffix *-ship* is used to form nouns like *scholarship*. Complete each sentence with an appropriate word from the list.

friendship	penmanship
leadership	scholarship
marksmanship	

1. The president of our country has guided this nation well; he's always been known for his qualities of _____ .
2. There was not a great _____ between Gloria Mitchem and the press.
3. If you want people to understand what you write, it's a good idea to improve your _____ .
4. The leader of our archery club hits the target every time; he's known for his _____ .
5. Susan can't afford to go to college with the little money she earned last summer, so she's applied for a _____ .

47. A risky business.

1. Have you ever made a decision about money that you now regret? If so, what should you have done differently?

 Julie Hart, a trainee, is talking with Sam Bradley, who has been a firefighter for ten years.

Listen to the conversation.

2

Julie Hi there, Sam.

Sam Hello, Julie . . . . By the way, I've been meaning to ask you something. Don't take it the wrong way. . . .

Julie Yes? What is it?

Sam Are you sure you belong in this program?

Julie Of course. Why shouldn't I be sure?

Sam Well, I'll be honest with you, Julie. Putting out fires is no job for a woman.

Julie We'll see about that, Sam! Besides, I enjoy firefighting. I feel as if I'm doing something really important for the people of this city.

Sam I heard you were in business school before this.

Julie Yes, but I dropped out during the second year. If I'd finished, I would have made a lot of money eventually. I'm happier doing this, though.

Sam Well, Julie, five years from now you'll be telling people, "I want to quit. I want to go back to something safer."

Julie Hmm. Would you ever quit, Sam?

Sam Sure I would. In fact, pretty soon I'll be staying home all the time, just counting my money. I won't be risking my life fighting fires.

Julie Oh, the lottery again. You're a dreamer, like everyone else here.

Sam No, I'm not. I don't waste my money on lottery tickets. I put my money into things I can see.

Julie Do you mean you invest your money in things like art?

Sam No, no. I mean real estate. Just old buildings like the ones around here. I've bought one already and plan to buy more. When I leave here, I'll really be making a lot of money.

Julie Don't quit your job yet, Sam. Real estate is a risky business.

Sam Hmm . . .

3. Say *Right, Wrong,* or *I don't know.*

1. Julie had been a business student.
2. None of Julie's friends think she should be a firefighter.
3. Julie plans to make a lot of money in business eventually.
4. Sam would like to quit his job.
5. Sam likes to play the lottery.
6. Julie will leave the fire department in five years.
7. Sam plans to make a good living in real estate.

48. I wonder what I'll be doing in five years.

1 ▶ **Look at the first picture and listen to the conversation.**
▶ **Act out similar conversations with a partner, using your own information or the other pictures.**

A My job is making me miserable. Selling sandwiches is no way to make a living.
B I know what you mean.
A I wonder what I'll be doing in five years.
B Don't worry. With your business sense, you'll be managing a chain of restaurants by then.

> In the future continuous, *will* (*'ll*) or *won't* is followed by *be* and a present participle.
> You'll be managing a restaurant.

2 ▶ **Study the frames: The future with *will* vs. the future continuous with *will***

The future			
I	'll	return	the camera at 3:30.
We	won't	have	jobs this summer.

The future continuous				
I	'll	be	taking	pictures until then.
We	won't		working	when we move.

The future

Use the future with *will* to talk about a specific event in the future.
  I*'ll* take your picture at 2:00.
  In twenty years, I*'ll* buy a house by the seashore.

Use the future with *will* with verbs such as *be, have, want*, and *like* to describe a future state.
  In twenty years, I*'ll* have a lot of money.

Use the future with *will* to talk about an event that will begin at the same time as another event.
  I*'ll* make dinner when you get home. (I'll start dinner then.)

The future continuous

Use the future continuous with *will* to talk about an ongoing activity in the future.
  I*'ll* be taking pictures all day.
  In twenty years, I*'ll* be living in a house by the seashore.

Use the future continuous with *will* to talk about an activity that will already be in progress when another event takes place.
  I*'ll* be making dinner when you get home. (I'll start dinner before then.)

3 ▶ **Listen to the conversation.**
▶ **Act out a similar conversation with a partner.**

A It's amazing how fast things change. I remember when I'd never even heard of computers.
B You know, I wonder what life will be like a hundred years from now.
A Well, maybe we'll be living on the moon . . . .
B I can just see it now. People will have their own rocket ships, and there will be traffic jams in outer space.

> Will there be . . .
>
> personal rocket ships?
> tiny, super-fast computers?
> one world language?
> trips to other planets?
> glass-covered cities?

4 ▶ Complete the following conversations with the future or the future continuous forms of the verbs in parentheses. Then listen to check your work.

1. **A** The show _____ (be) over at ten o'clock. Can you pick me up?
   B Sure. I _____ (wait) in the parking lot when you come out of the theater.

2. **A** I've never met Mr. Nelson, so how _____ I _____ (recognize) him at the train station?
   B Don't worry. He's a very tall, thin man, and he _____ a red jacket. (wear)

3. **A** One day we _____ (be) lucky and we _____ (win) the lottery.
   B You really think so?
   B Oh, sure. In twenty years, we _____ (work) anymore. We _____ (take) it easy.

4. **A** What do you think you _____ (do) a year from now?
   B Good question. I _____ (let) you know in a year.

5 ▶ Listen to the conversation.
   ▶ Act out similar conversations with a partner, using the information in the box. Give your true opinion.

A Would you ever play the lottery?
B If I had extra money, I would. Who knows? Maybe I'd be lucky . . . . Why? Would you?
A Me? Never. I think it's a waste of money.

> Would you ever . . .
>
> play the lottery?
> live in a very cold climate?
> have more than five children?
> take a flight to the moon?
> shake hands with a space creature?

6 ▶ Listen to the conversation.
   ▶ Complete the sentences.
   ▶ Act out conversations with a partner, discussing some of your regrets.

A You know, sometimes I'm sorry I went into business.
B Really? Don't you like what you're doing?
A Well, my job pays well, but it doesn't really interest me. If I'd gone to journalism school, I could have been a TV reporter.
B There's a lot of pressure in journalism, though . . . .

1. Sometime I'm sorry I _____ .
2. If I'd _____ , I would have been happier.
3. If I'd thought about it more, I wouldn't have _____ .
4. If I hadn't _____ , I wouldn't have _____ .
5. If I'd _____ , I could have _____ .

7 ▶ Listen to Terry talk to a friend about some things that are possibilities and other things that she regrets. Mark each illustration with *P* for possibility or *R* for regret.

8 ► **Study the frames: Contrary-to-fact conditional sentences**

Present time

If	Past tense form	Conditional		
	I had more money (I don't),	I **would** (I'd)	**buy**	a house.
	I were smart (I'm not),	I **wouldn't**	**play**	the lottery.
	he tried (he doesn't),	he **could**	**find**	a job.
	she weren't patient (she is),	she **couldn't**	**be**	a teacher.

▲
base form

Past time

If	Past perfect form	Past conditional		
	I'd had more money (I didn't),	I **would have**	**bought**	a house.
	I'd been smart (I wasn't),	I **wouldn't have**	**played**	the lottery.
	he'd tried (he didn't),	he **could have**	**found**	a job.
	she hadn't been patient (she was),	she **couldn't have**	**been**	a teacher.

▲
past participle

9 ► **Complete the sentences with the correct form of the verb in parentheses.**

1. I _____ (call) Ellen if I'd known her phone number.
2. If Sam _____ (live) closer, he wouldn't have been late.
3. If Dennis weren't so adventurous, he _____ (travel) so much.

4. If we _____ (finish) college, we'd have more job opportunities.
5. If he'd tried, Mr. Nelson _____ (got) to his son's baseball game.
6. If they _____ (be) here, the party would be more fun.

10 ► **Read the following situations. Then make a comment about each one with a present or past contrary-to-fact conditional sentence.**

1. The movie critics didn't like *Space Aliens*, but Cara didn't read the reviews. She went to see the movie with a friend and neither of them enjoyed it.
   If Cara had read the reviews, she wouldn't have gone to see the movie.
2. Carlos wants to retire, but he can't afford to. He would like to write his autobiography, but since he's still working, he doesn't have time.
3. Sarah always wanted to study architecture. Her parents told her it was a man's profession, so she became a teacher instead.
4. Toshio missed his plane because he got a flat tire on his way to the airport. He didn't have a spare tire in his trunk.
5. Denise went away on vacation without checking to see when her library books were due. When she returned them, she had to pay a large fine.

49. Your turn

You are faced with a difficult choice. You can either continue to live in the present, or you can choose to live in a futuristic community of the year 2100. This community has the features shown in these photos from science fiction movies. Study the photos carefully and read the information in the box. Then, working in groups, discuss what life will be like in the new community. What will your decision be? Here are some questions to consider:

1. Will changes in technology improve the quality of life?
2. How will people's values and ideas be different?
3. What new problems will people face? What will cause these problems?
4. Why will the futuristic community be a better or worse place in which to live?

Star Trek VI: The Undiscovered Country

Star Trek VI: The Undiscovered Country shows how there will always be problems in the search for intergalactic peace.

In the *Star Wars* trilogy, robots play an important part in a rebellion against the Evil Empire. R2D2 and C-3PO can think and act on their own. They become heroes in the war.

Alien Nation brings a group of space aliens to Earth, where they try to become part of society. The people of Earth must learn to overcome their fear and mistrust of the strangers.

In *Soylent Green*, the world is faced with overcrowding and a serious food shortage. New Yorkers of 2022 exist on meals of a food substitute whose main ingredients are soybeans, lentils, and a secret addition of recycled humans.

In the future of *Blade Runner*, it has become possible to make artificial people, called "replicants." The replicas have super strength and special talents but can live for only four years.

Star Wars

Alien Nation

Soylent Green

Blade Runner

📼 Listen in

Read the statements below. Then listen to a lecture by a futurologist, an expert on life in the future, and choose *a* or *b*.

1. The domes in the New Cities will _____ .
   a. protect people
   b. make it easier for people to travel

2. The weather in the New Cities will _____ .
   a. contain deadly meteor showers
   b. never be too wet or too cold.

3. The workday in the New Cities will be short because _____ .
   a. the sun will shine only a few hours a day
   b. computers will save a lot of time

4. The Earth will be important to New Cities inhabitants because _____ .
   a. they will return to live there soon
   b. they will be interested in the past

50. On your own

1. Work in groups to design and describe your own city or planet of the future.

2. You're a futurologist and have been asked to write a column for the magazine *New Directions*. Describe what you think life will be like in the year 2200.

PREVIEW

FUNCTIONS/THEMES	LANGUAGE	FORMS
Describe an embarrassing experience Suggest an alternative	Instead of watching where I was going, I was busy daydreaming. The next thing I knew, I was sitting right in a puddle of water. I just wanted to crawl into a hole and die. Instead of going dancing, why don't we go to the movies?	*Because, because of, in case, in case of,* and *instead of*
Express uncertainty	I couldn't decide whether or not to apologize.	*Whether* vs. *if*
Tell a joke Tell a story	Tell me whether or not I'm going crazy. When I was a child, I hated carrots. . . . I would feed our dog under the table. . . jl still don't know if my parents ever suspected it	

Preview the reading.

1. What do the illustrations below mean to you? Do these or other similar symbols exist in your culture? Discuss these questions with a partner.

2. Before you read the article on pages 110–111, look at the title and the illustrations. What do you think the article is about? Discuss your ideas with a partner.

51.

What Is This Thing Called

What is love?

Dr. Michael R. Liebowitz, assistant professor of clinical psychiatry at Columbia University, believes that falling in love is influenced by our brain chemistry. This connection between the way we feel and the way our bodies function is the focus of Dr. Liebowitz's book, *The Chemistry of Love*. In an interview with *People* magazine, Dr. Liebowitz discussed his neurochemical theories of romance.

♥ *Don't you find it upsetting to reduce an emotion like love to a chemical equation?*

I'm a big believer in romance. The emotions we feel when we're in love are so powerful that when they're going on, nobody's going to stop to think about chemicals in the brain. Look at it this way. I know how digestion works. I know what goes on in my body when I eat something. But that has nothing to do with my enjoyment of a good meal.

♥ *What is love, chemically speaking?*

I try to distinguish between romantic attraction and romantic attachment because I think they're chemically distinct. The symptoms of attraction—falling in love—

are very much like what happens when you take an artificial stimulant. Your heart beats faster, your energy goes up, you feel optimistic. There are certain chemicals in the brain—phenylethylamine (PEA) is one—that produce the same effect when released.

♥ *What, then, is the basis for romantic attachment? What keeps us together?*

There is an area in the lower brain called the *locus ceruleus*, where feelings of panic and separation anxiety seem to begin. There are certain brain chemicals, called endorphins, that slow down the activity of the *locus ceruleus*. I believe that we're programmed at birth to produce endorphins when we're in close relationships.

110 Unit 11

Love?

It's nature's way of keeping us together. When the relationship ends or when we're afraid that it might end, production of endorphins stops and we're thrown into a panic.

♥ *Why do people grow tired of each other?*

What's intense in a relationship is the newness. That's why the great romances of literature are never between people who stay together. Romeo and Juliet, for example, never had a chance to get used to each other.

♥ *Why does being in love make everything in life seem wonderful?*

Our pleasure centers need a minimum level of stimulation to function. Love lowers this level. When we're in love, it takes less stimulation to give us pleasure. That's why everything feels possible when you're in love, why everything looks rosy.

♥ *Do people work better when they're in love, or are they too distracted?*

When people's emotional needs are being met, they work better. Love gives you more energy, more enthusiasm.

♥ *How do you keep love alive? How do you keep the PEA flowing in your own ten-and-a-half-year marriage?*

You need newness, sharing, and growth. My wife changed careers lately. We shared that. She gave me a lot of ideas for this book. We were able to share that. We're buying a new home, an old farmhouse with some land. We'll be farmers together in a small way. All these shared changes are important. The brain has to experience a change, or there will be no excitement.

Figure it out

1. As you read the article, pay attention to the statements Dr. Liebowitz makes to define and describe love. When you have finished, decide which of these statements are correct according to him. Say *Right* or *Wrong*.

1. Romantic attachment is what people feel when they first fall in love.
2. Because of chemicals in the brain, falling in love can feel like taking an artificial stimulant.
3. Endorphins help to prevent separation anxiety.
4. People grow tired of each other when there is no newness to produce a chemical change in the brain.
5. When people are in love, they have trouble concentrating at work.

2. Answer the following questions.

1. What is Dr. Liebowitz's "neurochemical theory of romance"?
2. How are romantic attraction and romantic attachment chemically different?
3. What changes took place in the author's life that helped him keep love alive?

3. Say *Same* or *Different*.

1. pleasure
   enjoyment
2. optimistic
   depressed
3. attraction
   attachment
4. anxiety
   excitement
5. powerful
   very strong
6. effect
   result

4. The suffix *-ment* changes a verb into a noun, as in *enjoy* and *enjoyment*. First form nouns from the verbs in parentheses and fill in the blanks. Then complete each sentence appropriately.

1. The _____ (excite) in a relationship goes away if . . .
2. When children grow up, their _____ (attach) to their parents . . .
3. I had trouble hiding my _____ (disappoint) when . . .
4. The most boring _____ (assign) I ever had in school was . . .
5. A boss should give employees _____ (encourage) when . . .
6. . . . , but I haven't noticed any _____ (improve).
7. . . . gives me a lot of _____ (enjoy).

52. What a disaster!

1. Think of different things that would be embarrassing if they happened to you. Share your thoughts with a partner.

Melinda is telling her best friend, Miki, about her first date with Ray.

Listen to the conversation.

2

Miki	Hi, Melinda. Sorry I'm a little late.
Melinda	No problem. I'm just glad you could meet me for lunch.
Miki	So what happened on your date with Ray? Tell me about it!
Melinda	What a disaster! I was so embarrassed because of the way I looked. I had mud all over my dress.
Miki	How did *that* happen?
Melinda	Remember how it was pouring last night? Well, instead of watching where I was going, I was busy daydreaming. I tripped on a crack in the sidewalk, and the next thing I knew, I was sitting right in a puddle of water.
Miki	*(Laughs)* I'm sorry. I didn't mean to laugh.
Melinda	It may sound funny now, but it sure wasn't then. Poor Ray! He probably didn't know whether to laugh or cry.
Miki	Oh, Melinda, don't take it so hard. Just think, you and Ray will never forget your first date!
Melinda	If I ever hear from him again, that is.
Miki	Oh, I'm sure you will. Anyway, you haven't even told me what you did last night.
Melinda	Actually, we *did* see a pretty good movie. I guess you're right. It wasn't *all* bad . . . .

3. Choose *a* or *b*.

1. Melinda was embarrassed _____ her dress had mud on it.
   a. because
   b. because of

2. Melinda was daydreaming instead of _____ attention.
   a. paying
   b. to pay

3. Melinda fell down _____ a crack in the sidewalk.
   a. instead of
   b. because of

4. Ray probably didn't know _____ to laugh or cry.
   a. if
   b. whether

5. Miki didn't mean to laugh at Melinda's _____ experience.
   a. embarrassed
   b. embarrassing

6. Ray was probably a little _____ too.
   a. embarrassed
   b. embarrassing

53. Instead of watching where I was going ...

1 ▶ **Listen to the conversation.**
 ▶ **Act out a similar conversation with a partner. Think of an embarrassing experience you once had that seems humorous now. Share your experience with a partner.**

A I'll never forget my first date. It was pouring out, and instead of watching where I was going, I was busy daydreaming. I tripped on a crack in the sidewalk, and the next thing I knew, I was sitting right in a puddle of water.

B *(Laughs)* I'm sorry. I didn't mean to laugh.

A Oh, that's O.K. *(Laughs also)* It seems funny now, but at the time, I just wanted to crawl into a hole and die.

B I can imagine!

Some expressions
I was so embarrassed.
I felt my face getting red.
I just wanted to disappear.
I just wanted to crawl into a hole and die.

2 ▶ **Listen to the conversation.**
 ▶ **Complete the sentences.**
 ▶ **Work with a partner. Use the completed sentences in similar conversations. You've made plans to do something together. Now suggest alternatives to your plans.**

A Listen, I'm a little tired tonight. Instead of going dancing, why don't we go to the movies? There's a good movie playing at the Valencia Theater.

B That sounds fine. What time does it start?

A At 6:30, so let's meet in front of the theater at 6:15.

B Hmm . . . I have a meeting until 6:00. In case I'm late, go ahead and buy the tickets. I should definitely be there no later than 6:25.

1. Instead of going _____ , why don't we _____ ?
2. Instead of Friday, what if _____ ?
3. In case of rain, would you want to _____ ?
4. Because of the crowds, maybe we should _____ .
5. In case I'm late, _____ .
6. Let's _____ because _____ .

You've made plans to . . .
go dancing.
go to the beach.
go to a popular movie.

3 ▶ **Study the frame:**
 Because, because of, in case, in case of, and *instead of*

The picnic is canceled	**because**	it's raining.	sentence
	because of	the rain.	noun
Dial 911	**in case**	there's an emergency.	sentence
	in case of	an emergency.	noun
Let's take the car	**instead of**	going by bus.	gerund
		the bus.	noun

4 ▶ The Grants are going out for the evening and leaving their son, Henry, all alone for the first time. Complete the sentences with *because, because of, in case, in case of,* or *instead of*.

Mrs. Grant Now remember, _____ an emergency, call Mrs. Rivera. Here's her number.

Henry Oh, Mom, nothing's going to happen. Why don't you just relax _____ worrying about me all the time?

Mr. Grant We're just being practical, Henry. Now we want you to go to bed by 9:00 _____ school tomorrow. When we come home you should be sleeping.

Mrs. Grant And _____ it starts raining, make sure to close all the windows. Please don't forget _____ I don't want to find water on the floor when I come home.

Henry O.K. I won't forget. But _____ all these instructions, why don't you tell me what you left me for dinner?

5 ▶ Listen to the conversation.
▶ Think of a humorous situation in which you were unsure of what to do. Complete the sentences and use them to tell a classmate about your experience.

A I remember one time I was in an important meeting at work. I took off my sweater, and to my absolute horror a sock fell out!

B You're kidding! What did you do?

A Well, I didn't do anything. I couldn't decide whether or not to apologize. I mean, I wasn't sure if anyone had seen it. So I just picked up the sock as fast as I could and put it in my briefcase.

1. I couldn't decide whether (or not) to _____ .
2. I didn't know whether to _____ (or not).
3. I was wondering if I should _____ .
4. I had trouble making up my mind whether to _____ or _____ .
5. I wasn't sure if anyone _____ .

6 ▶ Study the frame: *Whether* vs. *if*

I can't decide	**whether**	(or not) to call him. to call him (or not). to call him or wait.	◀ *whether* + infinitive
	if **whether**	I should call him (or not). I should call him or wait.	◀ *if* or *whether* + sentence

7 ▶ Listen to the conversation and check (√) the pictures that show where the man and woman decide to go.

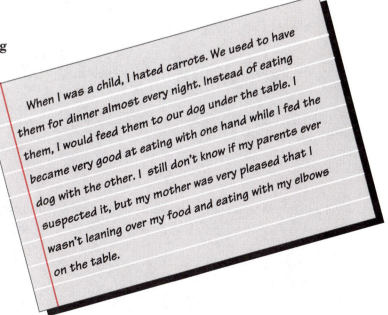

8 ▶ **Complete the jokes with *whether (or not)* or *if*. In some sentences, either one is correct.**

1.　"Doctor, you must help me!" said the patient to his psychiatrist. "Tell me _____ I'm going crazy. I can't seem to remember anything for more than a few minutes."

　　"How long has this been going on?" asked the psychiatrist.

　　"How long has what been going on?" replied the patient.

2.　"Oh, so you're the chief of police of this nice little town," the woman said. "I'm so pleased to meet you. I wonder _____ I could shake hands with the fire chief, too."

　　"Sure," the police chief answered. "Just wait until I change hats."

3.　An angry man charged into a jewelry shop and shook his new watch in the owner's face. "You said this watch would last a lifetime," he yelled.

　　The owner admitted, "I had trouble deciding _____ to tell you that. But you looked pretty sick the day you bought it."

4.　"I can't decide _____ to have a hamburger or a cheeseburger. Maybe you can help me." the customer said to the waiter.

　　"Sure I can. We're all out of cheese," the waiter replied.

9 ▶ **Think of a childhood prank you played on someone or something naughty that you did. Write a paragraph, explaining how you tried to fool the person or how you misbehaved.**

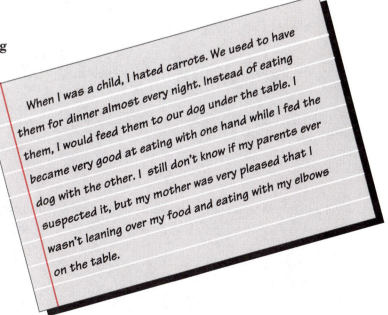

When I was a child, I hated carrots. We used to have them for dinner almost every night. Instead of eating them, I would feed them to our dog under the table. I became very good at eating with one hand while I fed the dog with the other. I still don't know if my parents ever suspected it, but my mother was very pleased that I wasn't leaning over my food and eating with my elbows on the table.

54. Your turn

One of the most popular forms of humor in many countries is the comic strip. Quino (Joaquin S. Lavado) was born in Mendoza, Argentina, and he created the cartoon strip *Mafalda*. Mafalda is the little girl in these cartoons, and the little boy, Guille, is her brother. Quino's cartoons have become world famous and have been translated into many languages. Work in groups to fill in the balloons, choosing the correct copy from the box below. Look at the artwork carefully, and discuss what details in the drawings add to the humor.

Mommy, was he your first boyfriend, or was someone else?

Good afternoon, what would you like?

And who are *you* thinking about, may I ask?!!!

All right! If you don't have soup, you don't get dessert!!

Will *everything* fit in here that they're going to teach me in school?

Good afternoon, what would you like?

But I only wanted to know if you were Mommy's first boyfriend . . .

How do you do? I just got here with my family, looking for some peace and quiet.

Listen, that's enough! Did you hear me? ENOUGH!!

I won't have any! I won't! I would be a disgusting person if there were some bribe that could make me sacrifice my principles, give up my beliefs, and betray my convictions!!

Good afternoon, I would like to speak to a grown-up . . .

How I hate myself sometimes!!

Just a minute.

Now isn't the time for questions! Get to bed!

Crêpes suzette . . .

📟 Listen in

Now look carefully at two more cartoon strips, both of which have somewhat serious themes. Listen to the conversations, and then, in your own words, write what each speaker is saying in each of the balloons.

What is the author's point of view in these two cartoon strips? Do you agree with his opinions? Discuss these questions in groups.

50. On your own

1. Write a composition, choosing one of the topics below.

1. Explain why you think Quino's cartoons on pages 116–117 have been so popular. What makes them appeal to people, and why are they humorous? Cite examples from the cartoons.
2. Discuss another humorist who has impressed you, and explain why you like this person's work. You may choose a cartoonist, a comedian, or an author. Cite specific examples of this person's humor.

2. Fill in the balloon for the cartoon below. Compare your words with a partner's. Then discuss with your partner what's funny about the cartoon.

P R E V I E W

FUNCTIONS/THEMES	LANGUAGE	FORMS
Report an event	"I was in the theater office," said Paulo Rodrigues. He said it was so dark that he needed a flashlight to find his way.	Direct speech vs. reported speech
Report a conversation	The captain told us to return to our seats.	
Talk about possibilities Make a judgment	Someone could have been killed. The traffic light should have been repaired a lot sooner.	The passive with modal auxiliaries in past time

Preview the reading.

1. What has happened in the picture below? What is such a disaster called? Compare your answers with a partner's answers.

2. Before you read the article on page 120, look at the title and the photos on pages 120–121. What do you think the article is about? Discuss your ideas with a partner.

56. WHOSE FAULT IS IT?

On January 17, 1994, an earthquake measuring 6.6 on the Richter scale changed the lives of people living near Los Angeles in the San Fernando Valley of southern California. The disaster left at least 55 people dead, destroyed or damaged thousands of homes, brought down major highways, and ruptured gas and water mains. The damage was estimated to be about $30 billion.

Even though the residents of California have always realized that earthquakes are a very real threat, most say going through one is an experience that you can't imagine until it's actually happened. At 4:31 A.M., the center of the quake was in Northridge, a neighborhood of garden apartments and shopping centers. Joan, a teacher, recalls waking up to a big rumble and the sound of her husband yelling, "It's the Big One!" She immediately ran toward her son's room. The walls were shaking and she screamed for him to run to the front door. They managed to escape safely, except for the cuts on Joan's bare feet. "There was broken glass everywhere," Joan said, "but I never felt it until I was together with my family outside and saw that my feet were bleeding." Her husband immediately started helping neighbors get out of their apartment building. After a couple of hours, he managed to get back into their apartment to grab some clothes and shoes. Joan's family will most likely be able to move back into their apartment because of the building's steel construction that allowed it to move and sway, but not cave in.

Not everyone was that fortunate. In one apartment complex that was not fortified with steel, the second and third floors collapsed onto the first floor, trapping and killing many residents. Emergency search-and-rescue teams were brought in to rescue any survivors. Guards were stationed to keep out those people who might risk their lives to go back in for possessions.

Could anyone have predicted this quake? For decades, people who live in California have been fearfully awaiting "The Big One," an earthquake along the San Andreas fault that could measure around 8.0 on the Richter scale. Southern California is an earthquake zone because it lies over faults, or cracks in the earth. Underneath the surface, the Earth's crust has separated into plates that are slowly trying to move past each other. In the areas where they can't pass, pressure builds, eventually erupting into an earthquake. The San Andreas fault is 800 miles long, and scientists have been monitoring it and measuring its movement in order to be able to predict a quake before it happens.

However, scientists realize that there are a large number of fault lines under the Earth, many of which are unknown to them. The aftershocks of the quake can give scientists some help in mapping out where these hidden fault lines are. Some quakes are preceded by foreshocks—rumbles that come before an earthquake. But there is no definite way to predict an earthquake. "We prefer the word *forecasting*," says one geologist. "It sounds like weather, which allows us to be wrong."

Figure it out

1. Read the article. Then mark the statements as follows: 1 = main idea; 2 = supporting detail; 0 = neither an idea nor a detail in this article.

1. ___ On January 17, 1994, an earthquake changed the lives of many people in southern California.
2. ___ Joan's family managed to escape safely from their apartment.
3. ___ Joan hid in her son's room before they escaped.
4. ___ Southern California is an earthquake zone.
5. ___ Scientists still cannot definitely predict an earthquake.
6. ___ The center of the quake was in Northridge.
7. ___ Scientists predicted the quake that happened in January of 1994.
8. ___ The San Andreas fault is 800 miles long.

2. Choose the correct ending for each of these sentences.

1. The earthquake of January 17, 1994, was caused by
   a. pressure that had built up between plates in the Earth's crust.
   b. the inaccurate predictions of scientists.

2. Scientists know that
   a. someone could have predicted the earthquake.
   b. before some earthquakes there are foreshocks.

3. Residents of southern California
   a. never seem to realize the true dangers of living over a fault.
   b. are very aware that earthquakes can take place where they live.

4. An unsafe building during an earthquake is one that
   a. has not been fortified with steel.
   b. moves and sways but doesn't collapse.

3. Match.

1. ruptured (adj.)   a. roar
2. rumble (n)   b. naked
3. bare (adj.)   c. exploding
4. grab   d. move back and forth
5. sway (v)   e. network
6. complex (n)   f. take
7. scale (n)   g. broken
8. erupting   h. instrument used to measure something

4. The highlighted words in the article are nouns that are used either as nouns or as adjectives to modify other nouns. Identify each of the highlighted words as either nouns (*n*) or adjectives (*a*). Then use each word in the opposite way in an original sentence.

57. Did you hear about the blackout?

1. **Discuss one of these topics with a partner.**

1. Have you ever joined a crowd that has gathered because of an accident, a fire, or a crime? What questions did you ask, and what did you find out?
2. Have you ever known anyone who has experienced a hurricane, an earthquake, or another type of natural disaster? What did the person tell you about his or her experience?

 Celia is talking to her friend Phyllis during a coffee break at work.

Listen to the conversation.

2

Celia	Hi, Phyllis. Any coffee left?
Phyllis	Sure. Help yourself.
Celia	Did you hear about the blackout downtown last night?
Phyllis	Yes, someone told me you were stuck in it.
Celia	Not me—Paulo. He was in the theater office when all the lights suddenly went out. It was so dark that he had to use a flashlight to find his way.
Phyllis	Really? People must have gone crazy. Did everyone panic?
Celia	Fortunately, no. Paulo said people were mad because the movie had stopped, though. They kept asking if they were going to get their money back.
Phyllis	No kidding! What did he do?
Celia	About the money? He promised them refunds.

Phyllis	No, I mean in general.
Celia	Oh, well, he explained what had happened and told everyone to please stay seated.
Phyllis	That was smart. Someone could have been trampled, otherwise.
Celia	Oh, Paulo was very careful. He had the ushers lead the people out one by one.
Phyllis	It all sounds pretty unpleasant to me. You know, I heard on the radio that the power didn't come back on until this morning.
Celia	Did they say what had caused the blackout?
Phyllis	No, but it must have been caused by the heat. I'll bet every air conditioner in town was on last night.

3. **Say *Same* or *Different*.**

1. He told people to stay seated.
   He told people not to get up.

2. They kept asking him why the movie had stopped.
   Somebody asked him why the movie had stopped.

3. It must have been caused by the heat.
   The heat must have caused it.

4. I heard that the power didn't come back on until this morning.
   I heard that the power hadn't come back on yet this morning.

5. Someone could have been injured, otherwise.
   Someone was probably injured.

58. She said that there was a blackout.

1 ► Study the frames: Direct speech vs. indirect speech

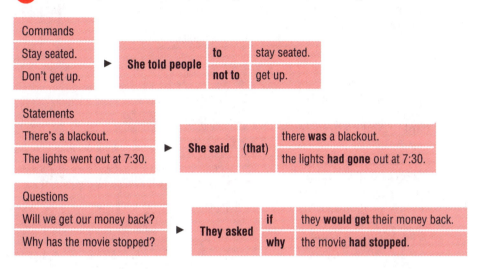

Commands

| Stay seated. | ► She told people | **to** | stay seated. |
| Don't get up. | | **not to** | get up. |

Statements

| There's a blackout. | ► She said | (that) | there **was** a blackout. |
| The lights went out at 7:30. | | | the lights **had gone** out at 7:30. |

Questions

| Will we get our money back? | ► They asked | **if** | they **would get** their money back. |
| Why has the movie stopped? | | **why** | the movie **had stopped**. |

2 ► Listen to the conversation.
► Read the newspaper articles. Tell another student about the events in them.

A Hey, did you hear about the blackout last night?

B No, I didn't. What happened?

A Well, it seems the entire downtown area was without lights. They interviewed the manager of a movie theater. He said it was so dark that he needed a flashlight to find his way.

B I'm glad I didn't go to the movies last night. I would have been furious.

A People were. They kept asking if they were going to get their money back . . .

> Why *has* the movie *stopped?* → They asked why the movie *had stopped.*
> Did people *panic?* → A reporter asked if people *had panicked.*

> When verbs that refer to states, such as *be* or *want,* are in the past tense in direct speech, use a past tense form in indirect speech.
>
> *Were* people angry? → He asked if people *were* angry.
> Why *did* people *want* their money back? → She asked why people *wanted* their money back.

Some expressions

People	asked . . .
	kept asking . . .
	said . . .
	wondered . . .
	wanted to know . . .
The manager	told them . . .
	said . . .
	explained . . .
	assured them . . .

Clinton Neighborhood News

■ Heat Wave Is Probable Cause of Blackout

Investigators believe that this week's heat wave must have caused the massive blackout in the downtown area last night. Power was not restored in a three-mile area until 9:00 this morning.

"I was in the theater office," said Paulo Rodrigues, manager of Cinema 3. "All of a sudden the lights went out. It was so dark that I needed a flashlight to find my way."

"Luckily, no one panicked," Rodrigues told reporters, "but people were angry. They kept asking two questions over and over: 'Why has the movie stopped?' and 'Are we going to get our money back?'"

■ Citizen Cheered for Catching Purse Snatcher

Neil Franklin has become something of a local hero after recovering an elderly woman's purse from a thief on Market Street late yesterday afternoon.

"This is a very small town, and there's never been an incident like this around here," said eighty-year-old Beverly Walker, whose purse was snatched by a twenty-year-old man as she was crossing the street.

"My only thought was to help her," said Mr. Franklin, who was inside a store when he heard the woman cry for help. "So I went up to her and asked some questions: 'What does he look like?, What is he wearing?'—that sort of thing. She was very upset, but I told her, 'Stay calm. I'll get him.' And then I ran after him and caught him."

People cheered Franklin when he brought the thief to police headquarters.

3 ▶ **During a recent plane trip, you were seated near a very nervous teenager. Report her conversation with a flight attendant, changing direct speech to reported speech.**

Captain	The seat belt sign has been turned on. Please return to your seats.
Teenager	Ooh! Is the plane going to crash?
Flight Attendant	Of course it isn't. This is simply a routine procedure. Everything is fine.
Teenager	Then why did the captain tell us to fasten our seat belts?
Flight Attendant	Please don't worry. We've run into a little bad weather, but it won't be a problem.
Teenager	Are you just trying to make me feel better?
Flight Attendant	No, really, there isn't any problem. Just try to relax.
Teenager	Oh. Well, then, when can I take off my seat belt?
Flight Attendant	You can take it off as soon as the light overhead goes off.
Teenager	Thank you. This isn't so bad after all.

There was a very nervous teenage girl near me on the plane. It must have been her first flight. When the captain told us to return to our seats, she asked the flight attendant if the plane was going to crash. The flight attendant told her that it wasn't. . . .

 4 ▶ **Listen to the news broadcast and number the drawings in the correct order.**

124 Unit 12

5 ▶ **Study the frames: The passive with modal auxiliaries in past time**

Active				
They	should		arrested	the driver.
They	could would	have	prevented	the accident.
The driver	may might		injured	someone.
They	must		called	the police.

▲ past participle

◀

a judgment	
a result	
a possibility	
a logical conclusion	

▶

Passive				
The driver	**should**			**arrested.**
The accident	**could** **would**	have	been	**prevented.**
Someone	**may** **might**			**injured.**
The police	**must**			**called.**

▲ past participle

6 ▶ **Read the newsbriefs and listen to the conversation.**
  ▶ **Act out similar conversations with a partner. Discuss the possible causes of the incidents.**

A There was a traffic accident at the corner of Maple Street and Tenth Avenue yesterday. A truck hit a school bus.
B That's awful. Was anyone hurt?
A Fortunately, no, but someone could have been killed. The traffic light has been broken for a week.
B Is that what caused the accident?
A Well, it's hard to say. It might have been caused by drunken driving.

7 ▶ **Listen to the conversation.**
  ▶ **Act out similar conversations with a partner.**
  ▶ **Make judgments about the incidents you discussed in exercise 6.**

A It's a good thing no one was hurt in that accident at Maple and Tenth. The traffic light should have been repaired a lot sooner.
B I agree. And if the driver was drunk, he should have been arrested.

8 ▶ **Respond to each situation with a passive sentence about the past, using a modal auxiliary.**

1. The feeder at the zoo was surprised when Bobo the gorilla wouldn't eat anything. There were already banana peels all over his cage.
2. Robert and Cathy Charles went out to dinner. When they returned, the lock on the front door of their house was broken and their television and VCR were gone.
3. Ten-year-old Jason Peritz broke his foot in gym class and was taken to the hospital. When Jason didn't come home from school at the normal time, his mother was frightened. No one had told her what happened.
4. A car parked on Elm Street rolled down the hill yesterday afternoon. Fortunately, no one was hurt.

Newsbriefs

MIDLAND, OKLA.—A truck carrying auto parts collided with a school bus at the corner of Maple Street and Tenth Avenue yesterday at 4:32 P.M. No one was injured, but both vehicles were seriously damaged. Area residents reported that the traffic light at the corner had been broken since last Tuesday. The truck driver was suspected of drunken driving, but he was not arrested.

NORTHFIELD, W. VA.—A West Virginia mine has been closed for inspection after an explosion yesterday morning trapped ten miners for over nine hours. A rescue squad was not called until two hours after the explosion because officials said they did not know that anyone was missing. Miners at the Ridgewood Mine in Northfield had complained repeatedly about poor safety over the last several months. The mine has not been inspected regularly, and engineers are now looking into the possibility of a gas leak.

GORILLA

59. Your turn

Work with a group and study one set of illustrations. Then choose one of the illustrations and report on it to a group of classmates who looked at the other set. Imagine that you witnessed the event and talked with many other people at the scene. Answer these questions.

1. What exactly happened? Did everyone who witnessed the event agree? Did the newspapers give the same description?
2. What do you think caused the incident?
3. How could the incident have been prevented?
4. Is there anything that should have been done that wasn't?

Here are some words you may want to use: *elephant, escape (v), zoo, tent, statue, flood (n, v), laundry basket.*

Here are some words you may want to use: *scatter, bucket, paint (n, v), spill, gun, mask.*

🔊 Listen in

Read the paragraph below. Then listen to the conversation between two neighbors and complete the paragraph.

    Mrs. Harrison was upset because a(n) _____ had tried to _____ into her house. The _____ had escaped from the _____ but was finally _____ around 4:30. The _____ assured the Harrison family that the incident was very unusual.

60. On your own

1. Listen to each description as you look at the corresponding picture. Write a report on what was said, changing direct speech to reported speech.

He said he was getting concerned about all the lightning. He said . . .

2. Write a short news story. Report on an event that you have personally witnessed or an interesting event that you have heard or read about.

Review of units 7-12

1 ▶ As you read the article, try to figure out what the words *grunge*, *thrift shop*, and *runway* mean. (Hint: *Grungy* is a word you'll find in most English dictionaries.) When you've finished reading, decide which sentence below best expresses the meaning of the title.

a. The grunge fashion started with the use of thrift-shop clothes and ended up with high-priced designer clothes used on fashion-show runways.

b. Grunge music gave way to the grunge fashion of wearing flannel at local thrift shops and at airport runways.

Hair: The Latest Twist

So, you've got your grunge outfit picked out, and now you're trying to figure out what to do with your hair. . . . Why not try a braid? It could be a long one down the middle of your back or, even more popular, a few small braids of varying lengths around your head. This works well with the natural look in makeup and new, easy clothes. Braids don't have to be perfect—in fact, one New York hairstylist describes the look as "controlled messy."

2 ▶ Read these questions. Then scan the article to answer them.

1. Where does the grunge fashion in clothes come from?
2. How would you describe the original grunge style in clothes?
3. What's the difference between "thrift-shop grunge" and "runway grunge"?
4. How does Jeff Ament feel about "runway grunge"?
5. What does "controlled messy" mean?

Grunge: From the Thrift Shop to the Runway

Music has always influenced fashion, especially among teenagers and young adults. In the late 1980s and early 1990s, Seattle, Washington, was home to a new sound—grunge—that came out of garages and small clubs. Rock music by bands like Nirvana, Pearl Jam, and Soundgarden became the rage. The Seattle sound was loud, and the look was down-to-earth, affordable, and not at all flashy. As the music became more popular, so did copying the style of the musicians. This translated to fashion that mixes work clothes like flannel shirts and long johns with vintage clothes from thrift shops. These layers of old clothing are topped off with hats: thin, crocheted caps, baseball caps, or long stocking caps, for example. Shoes are chosen for comfort, not style; in fact, they are more likely to be heavy combat boots.

Fashion designers are often influenced by pop culture, so it didn't take long for the grunge look to make it to the runway—at much higher prices than at your local thrift shop! Jeff Ament, a member of Pearl Jam, has this comment to make: "It's a bunch of fashion people jumping on the bandwagon. "What a brilliant idea; we'll market a bunch of flannel shirts and crazy shorts and we'll make a mint." And at this point, a lot of people, myself included, won't even wear flannel because it's this total hip thing."

3 ► **Complete the pararaph with the correct quantifiers.**

_____ (Many/Much) trends in pop culture affect _____ (a lot of/a little) young people. For example, _____ (many/much) pop music has had a direct influence on _____ (much/many) young people's lives. _____ (Many/Much) fashion designers are also influenced by pop culture, and they create _____ (some/much) of the new fashions in clothes to fit a particular trend. _____ (A few/A little) older people also buy the latest pop fashion designs, but they probably don't wear them _____ (much/many) of the time.

4 ► **Magazine writer Maureen Williams is talking with clothes designer Marti Sandoval. Complete their conversation with the future or the future continuous forms of the verbs in parentheses.**

Williams What are your plans for next spring's collection?

Sandoval Actually, I'm not answering any questions yet. *(Laugh)* You _____ (get) your answer next month when my catalogue is ready.

Williams Well, I _____ (wait) for it! Tell me, how do you get ideas for new styles?

Sandoval Well, I just watch what people are wearing. For example, I _____ (be) in France and Italy next month, and I _____ (look) for new ideas the whole time. If I see anything exciting, I _____

_____ (make) a drawing of it right away. And I always plan well ahead of time. By the time you receive my spring catalogue, I _____ (work) on designs for next winter.

Williams How about the future? How are styles going to change over the next twenty years?

Sandoval I think styles _____ (become) more conservative. People _____ (spend) their money on computers instead.

5 ► **Sally is the adventurous type, but her friend Janet doesn't like anything new or different. Complete Janet's responses, using a sense verb and *like*, *as if*, or *as though* in your answers.**

1. **Sally** Cindy's braids are certainly interesting.
   Janet I don't think so. _____ .

2. **Sally** Listen They're playing the new Bruce Taylor album.
   Janet You call that music? _____ .

3. **Sally** Isn't that a terrific painting of a mother and child?
   Janet Is that what it is? _____ .

4. **Sally** Here, try this caviar omelet. It's delicious.
   Janet Ugh! _____ .

5. **Sally** Isn't the guest speaker interesting?
   Janet I don't think so. _____ .

6 ▶ Before you read the article, try to figure out what the title means. Then read the article. When you have finished reading, explain the title in your own words.

SPECIAL AILMENTS CAN SILENCE THE MUSIC

BY BARBARA ZIGLI

While athletes worry about tennis elbow and jogger's knee, musicians have their own set of problems: horn player's palsy, fiddler's neck, cymbal player's shoulder, and flutist's chin.

At best, those problems are a temporary annoyance that can lower the quality of a top performance. At worst, they ruin a musical career.

"There isn't a lot in the medical literature about these things," says Dr. Richard Lederman of the Cleveland Clinic. "The area is where sports medicine was 15-20 years ago—just beginning to draw some interest."

To encourage that interest, the Cleveland Clinic and Music Associates of Aspen (Colorado) are co-sponsoring a conference on "Medical Problems of Musicians," in Aspen.

"When we talk about musicians, we're talking about millions of people, from school kids to the adult amateur to the professional," says Dr. Howard L. Levine, a Cleveland Clinic specialist in nasal, sinus, and throat problems.

Most musicians report some physical problems, Lederman says, and most can be treated or cured with physical therapy, exercise, and medication.

Common ailments include:
- Tightness of the lips and facial muscles among horn players.
- Skin lesions on the necks of violin and viola players.
- Finger numbness or a facial rash from flute playing.
- Pain and tightness in the upper arms of cymbal players.
- Enlargement of the throat or temporary paralysis of the soft palate of woodwind players.
- Hearing loss among musicians sitting near the percussion section.
- And the dreaded Diplacusis, a hearing disorder that causes a musician to hear two different tones when a single tone is played.

7 ▶ Complete the statements below with *because, because of, in case, in case of,* or *instead of.* Then skim the article again and say *Right, Wrong,* or *I don't know* for each statement.

1. A musician's career may be ruined _____ health problems.
2. To prevent health ailments, young people should choose stringed instruments like the violin _____ playing wind instruments like the flute or horn.
3. _____ a muscle injury, a musician should first consult a physical therapist.
4. A musician with Diplacusis hears two notes _____ one.
5. There isn't much to read on the health problems of musicians _____ doctors are just becoming interested in the subject.

8 ► Oliver Davis recently started taking violin lessons, and he's developed a painful blister on his finger. Restate the nurse's part of the conversation, changing the sentence in brackets [ ] to the passive. Omit the agent where it isn't necessary.

Nurse [You should cover this blister] until it heals.

Oliver So I can't take the bandage off at all?

Nurse No, except that [you must change it once a day.] Also, [you should apply this cream] once a day.

Oliver Can I practice the violin?

Nurse No, because [it might irritate the blister.]

Oliver But I'll forget how to play!

Nurse Oh, [the cream will heal the blister] in less than a week.

Oliver I hope I won't get another blister when I start to play again. Oh, by the way, I have an appointment next Thursday, but I'm going out of town that day.

Nurse Just talk to the receptionist. I'm sure [she can change your appointment] to Wednesday.

9 ► Greg is a cymbal player whose arms are killing him, and he's having trouble doing his job at a grocery store. Give the manager's responses to Greg's statements, using the causative *get* or the causative *have* in either active or passive sentences.

Greg These boxes are in the way, and I don't think I can move them.

Manager _____ .

Greg I'd really appreciate it. Uh, those bottles of juice that were just delivered—I don't think I can carry them, either.

Manager Well, Steve's here today. _____ .

Greg I'm afraid I'm going to have trouble putting those jars on the top shelves, too.

Manager I'm sure Shelly wouldn't mind helping out. _____ .

Greg Wasn't I supposed to put up new signs in the windows today?

Manager Yes, but don't worry. _____ .

Greg Oh, thank you. This has never happened to me before. I can't even drive my car!

Manager You mean you walked here! _____ . If I can't find anyone, I'll drive you home myself.

 10 ► Kenneth, a make-up artist, is talking to Ruth, a singer, before a rehearsal for a TV show. Read the questions below. Then listen to the conversation and answer the questions..

1. What are Ruth's two health problems? Which one is worrying her and why?
2. If Kenneth had the same two health problems, which one would cause him a lot of trouble at work? Why?

11 ▶ Before you read the article, look at the illustration and the title and try to figure out what the article is about. Then read the article. When you have finished reading, explain the title in your own words.

A VOICE FROM THE PAST

When a German couple noticed a man's head and shoulder sticking out of a glacier in the Austrian Alps recently, they made history. The frozen corpse was about five feet tall, and scientists who helicoptered to the site determined that it was 4,000 years old—the first intact body ever found from the Bronze Age. Mummified by the wind and snow, he came complete with skin, bones, internal organs, and fingernails. He was dressed in leather shoes and a finely stitched leather suit, insulated with hay. An array of weapons and equipment was found alongside him—including a leather quiver with fourteen arrows, a stone necklace, a fire flint, a knife, and an ax with a crude bronze head.

"The find is of extraordinary scientific meaning," said Konrad Spindler, professor of Early and Primeval History at the University of Innsbruck, who is investigating the discovery. Skeletal remains of buried corpses have been excavated before in Bronze Age graves. But "the Iceman," as Austrian newspapers dubbed him, was going about the normal course of life when he died between the ages of 20 and 40, which means he should yield a treasure-trove of information about conditions 4,000 years ago. Scientists plan to study the contents of his stomach and intestine for clues to the Bronze Age diet, illnesses, and parasites. They also hoped to search the glacier site further for companions.

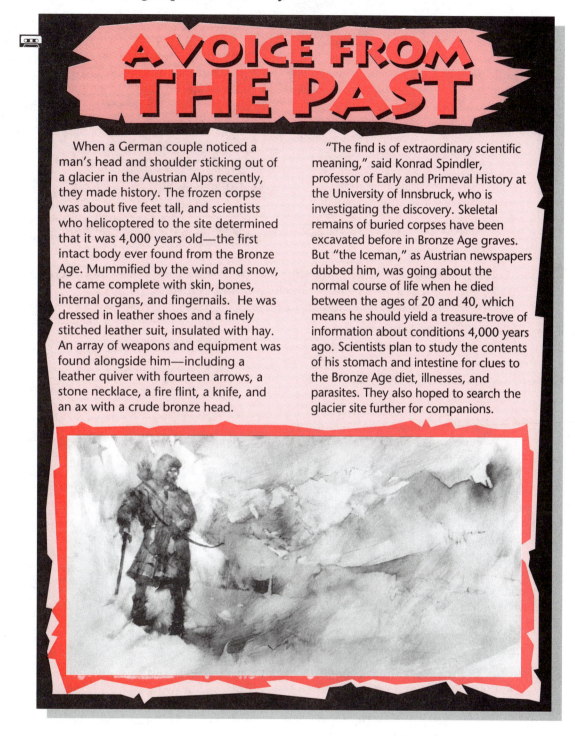

12 ▶ Rewrite this summary of the story, putting the sentences in brackets into the passive and omitting the agent where it isn't necessary.

[A German couple made history.] They discovered a frozen corpse of a man in a glacier in the Austrian Alps. [Scientists have determined the age of the corpse]—he appears to be 4,000 years old! [The elements have mummified the body of the man and preserved and his clothes.] [The scientists also found weapons alongside the corpse.] [Austrian newspapers dubbed the man "the Iceman,"] and he should provide scientists with a lot of information about conditions 4,000 years ago.

13 ▸ Complete the article about the newspaper survey with appropriate quantifiers, comparatives of quantifiers, or quantifiers with *of*. Some items have more than one answer.

The men and women we talked to participated in _____ outdoor activities this summer. _____ required special equipment, but _____ didn't—hiking. _____ men _____ women went canoeing; however, _____ women went camping _____ men. _____ men _____ women went hot-air ballooning. _____women were also enthusiastic hikers and campers, and _____ went mountain-climbing and canoeing as well.

What outdoor activities did you do this summer?		
	MEN	WOMEN
mountain climbing	5	3
hiking	4	5
canoeing	7	2
camping	6	6
hot-air ballooning	1	8

14 ▸ Leon Baker and Pat Martin are supposed to go camping in the mountains with some friends. Leon's never been camping before. Report his conversation with Pat, changing direct speech to reported speech.

Leon I'm a little nervous about the trip.
Pat Don't worry. Everything will work out fine.
Leon Have you ever gone camping there before? How do you know it's safe?
Pat My brother has been there twice, and I've seen all his photos. It's a beautiful place—safe and comfortable.
Leon But . . . are there bears?
Pat They won't come near us unless we leave food out. Please, stop worrying so much!
Leon I'm sorry. I can't help it, but I'll try to relax.

> When a sentence has more than one verb, the form of each verb changes in reported speech:
> *I'm sure* it's safe. → He said he *was sure* it *was safe*.

15 ▸ Roy Collins went mountain climbing in the Alps. One of the boots he was wearing came apart during his climb, and now he's complaining to the manager of the store where he bought the boots. Restate the conversation, putting the sentences in brackets [ ] in the passive and omitting the agent where it isn't necessary.

Roy [Someone should have inspected these boots.] I'm lucky to be alive!
Manager Sir, [someone must have inspected them] at the factory.
Roy Well, [they must not have done it] very carefully. Just look at the condition of this boot; the heel is very loose.
Manager Well, [a rock might have caused the damage].
Roy Then [someone should have designed these boots] better. Boots for mountain climbing are supposed to be very strong. [That accident could have killed me!]
Manager Just let me write down your name. . . .

16 ▶ Read the title and the first paragraph of the article. Can you predict what the rest of the article will be about? Write down your answer. Then read the article and change your answer if necessary.

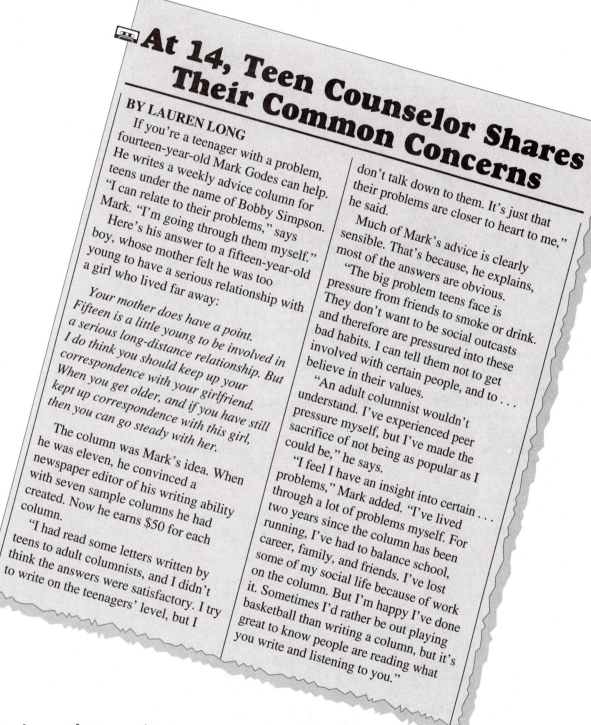

At 14, Teen Counselor Shares Their Common Concerns

BY LAUREN LONG

If you're a teenager with a problem, fourteen-year-old Mark Godes can help. He writes a weekly advice column for teens under the name of Bobby Simpson. "I can relate to their problems," says Mark. "I'm going through them myself."

Here's his answer to a fifteen-year-old boy, whose mother felt he was too young to have a serious relationship with a girl who lived far away:

Your mother does have a point. Fifteen is a little young to be involved in a serious long-distance relationship. But I do think you should keep up your correspondence with your girlfriend. When you get older, and if you have still kept up correspondence with this girl, then you can go steady with her.

The column was Mark's idea. When he was eleven, he convinced a newspaper editor of his writing ability with seven sample columns he had created. Now he earns $50 for each column.

"I had read some letters written by teens to adult columnists, and I didn't think the answers were satisfactory. I try to write on the teenagers' level, but I don't talk down to them. It's just that their problems are closer to heart to me," he said.

Much of Mark's advice is clearly sensible. That's because, he explains, most of the answers are obvious.

"The big problem teens face is pressure from friends to smoke or drink. They don't want to be social outcasts and therefore are pressured into these bad habits. I can tell them not to get involved with certain people, and to ... believe in their values.

"An adult columnist wouldn't understand. I've experienced peer pressure myself, but I've made the sacrifice of not being as popular as I could be," he says.

"I feel I have an insight into certain problems," Mark added. "I've lived through a lot of problems myself. For two years since the column has been running, I've had to balance school, career, family, and friends. I've lost some of my social life because of work on the column. But I'm happy I've done it. Sometimes I'd rather be out playing basketball than writing a column, but it's great to know people are reading what you write and listening to you."

17 ▶ Answer these questions.

1. What are Mark Godes's main reasons for writing a column for teenagers.
2. According to Mark, what is one big problem teenagers face? What did Mark do when he was faced with this problem himself?
3. Why does Mark feel he's a good columnist for teenagers?
4. If you were a teenager with a problem and wanted advice, would you write to Mark or to an adult columnist? Why?

18 ▶ Rewrite this teenager's letter to an advice columnist, changing the sentences in brackets to present or past contrary-to-fact conditional sentences.

Start like this:

Dear Nancy,

If I didn't have a little sister, I would be a lot happier. . . .

Dear Nancy,

[I'm not very happy, and the reason is my little sister.] For example, last night I was talking on the phone instead of doing my homework. My little sister was listening at the door. [I got in trouble only because she told my parents.] I think she actually wanted to see me get punished.

Last week I failed a math test, but I didn't show it to my parents. [Nobody knew about it until my little sister looked through my papers.] Of course she told my parents.

I don't think this is fair. [She keeps telling on me because my parents always take her side.] What should I do?

The brat's brother

19 ▶ Complete the conversation between two teenagers with *whether* or *if*.

Andrea What are you going to do this summer?

Terry I haven't decided _____ to work at the grocery store or take care of people's yards. How about you?

Andrea To tell you the truth, I don't know _____ I should work at all this summer. I've had so much trouble with math this year. I'm still trying to decide _____ or not to go to summer school.

Terry Well, it's up to you. Personally, I'm not sure _____ I could stand going to school in the summer.

20 ▶ Read the advice column. Then rewrite the article, changing the sentences in brackets [ ] to the passive and omitting the agent where it isn't necessary.

Dear Dr. Lee:
I've looked everywhere for an after-school job with no luck. Any suggestions?
—Frustrated

Dear Frustrated:
Many teenagers have written to me on this topic. Perhaps you will get some ideas from Carol Janus, who was interviewed by the Bedford Democrat. *I've reprinted the article, with permission of that paper.*

An Enterprising Young Woman
Meet Carol Janus. She is only thirteen years old, but [she has already planned her future.] She wants to be a veterinarian, own her own home, and have at least two horses. [Someone will have to pay her college tuition,] and Carol has already begun to save.

[Companies can't hire boys and girls who are under sixteen years of age,] so Carol looked for work around the neighborhood. She knew that [nobody needed one more baby sitter,] and she discovered that [kids had taken all the paper routes.]

As a result, Carol decided to start her own service as a plant-and-pet sitter. Now when people go on trips, they call Carol ["No one has done anything like this] around here before," said one happy client. "Many plants might have died and [people would have put the pets] in a kennel. Now [someone waters the plants,] and [someone takes care of the pets] at home."

Carol Janus is not just a dreamer. She is doing something to make dreams come true.